THE NEW WORLD BEGINS

THE NEW WORLD BEGINS

(The Truth behind Mayan and Other Predictions)

Dr. Bindya HSB Singh

Library of Congress, March 2013

GYAN

ISBN: 978-81-212-1238-0

Price: ₹ 250

First Published, 2015

Published by

Gyan Publishing House
23, Main Ansari Road
Daryaganj, New Delhi-110002
Phones: 23282060, 23261060
Fax: 91-11-23285914
E-mail: books@gyanbooks.com

Laser Typesetting: Gyan Print (AB-I)

Printed at: Chawla Offset Printers, Delhi

Cataloging in Publication Data—DK
Courtesy: D.K. Agencies (P) Ltd. <docinfo@dkagencies.com>

BHS, *Dr.,* **author.**
The new world begins : the truth behind Mayan and other predictions / Dr. BHS.
pages cm
Includes bibliographical references (pages).
ISBN 9788121212380

1. End of the world. 2. Two thousand twelve, A.D. 3. Mayas—Prophecies. 4. Mayas—Antiquities. 5. Chicheìn Itzaì Site (Mexico). I. Title.

DDC 972.81016 23

Contents

The End of the World has been predicted repeatedly by many for thousands of years.

And as the old world ends, the New World begins.

None of us have a choice but to accept the transformation and learn to rejoice with the change!

The Mayan Site in Chichen Itza on 12/22/12.

Acknowledgements

I would like to convey my sincere thanks to my parents, family, teachers, students, colleagues and friends for bearing with me and supporting me through challenging times.

In particular, I thank my parents for their agape love and acceptance of all faiths. My gratitude to school principal Sir Din Dayal for daily prayers in assembly, Mrs Bruno for gifting me my first cross at age of ten, Dr Hussain for teaching me the beginning prayer of *Qur'an*, Mr and Mrs Bhatia for their spiritual Hindu life-style and teachings, and my Sikh, Jewish and Buddhist friends for sharing their spiritual paths.

I salute my three guardian angels, Dorothy Stewart, Cecilia Lopez and Gail Forde, devout Christians, for praying with me so often with complete sincerity and showering their unconditional love. In so doing, they helped me realise a whole new world, the magical world of God's power.

I would also like to express my gratitude to Pastor Tim Wood, and Virginia Oparowski for sharing their love and passion for God through *Jesus Christ*; HG Vaisesika, Akruranath and Raxit Prabhujis for sharing their wisdom and devotion to God through *Lord Krishna*. A very special thanks to Dr Mazhar Khan, Dr Kanwaljit Bhatia, Sudha Tomar for reviewing contents of the book at short notice.

And above all, I bow with complete obedience and obeisance to that Supreme Power, the Universal Eternal Infinite Blissful Energy that has turned my life inside out with the eternal wisdom and realisation of our true identity and the pure feeling of peace, joy, love, wisdom, strength and self-contentment.

The book would not have been in a presentable form without the help of the following:

Content Editor : *Ms Sumedha Singh*
Language Editor : *Ms Shivali Singh*
Designing : *Mr Sohil S Singh*
Layout : *Dr S.K. Singh.*

The Entry Ticket to Mayan Site in Chichen Itza.

Introduction

It appeared to be purely coincidental that our family landed on the grounds of the Mayan Village, Chichen Itza, about 200 km from Cancun, the day after the world was supposed to 'end' as per their (*Mayan*) prediction. But it had to be more than just a mere coincidence, since my quest for universal wisdom had come to a peak. For the last several years, I had been tossed by fate to search for a higher wisdom and the intensity had reached a peak in the last few months following an unbelievable turn of events in my life.

But I had not even dreamt of ever probing the insights offered by Mayan philosophy and beliefs. However, winter of 2012 brought our family to desire a warm break. Our friends suggested Cancun in Mexico as a beautiful location, and we stumbled upon an enticing deal for four days. Two days before our departure, our oldest child sent us her request from Los Angeles to visit X-Caret theme park and Chichen Itza village, of which we had never heard of before. The way the arrangements materialised, we landed on the spiritual Mayan village about 12 hours after the prediction of the "End of World" deadline.

Oblivious to what destiny was unfolding, we checked into Hotel Royal Mayan on 20th December, 2012 and interestingly were allocated to suite number L444 (#4 has been associated with prophecy in some beliefs)! The next day we explored X-Caret and experienced strong gusty winds at night, as if reminding us that something significant was on its way. On December 22nd, we took the two and a half hour, bus ride to the historic city with the Mayan village preserves, Chichen Itza.

On that sunny and peaceful day, the air was crisp and grounds alive with the buzz of human energy. The serenity of the sacred site was well-preserved by the empirical monuments, despite the humble and unassuming land. The majestic pyramidal shaped temple, with its steep steps and symbolic snake and lion figurate, was an amazing sight to behold. The expansive playground and sculptured walls seemed to be still whispering historical values. The teeming crowds, curiously inspecting and searching for answers, were positioned around knowledgeable guides. It appeared that they all were synchronously tuning into ancient wisdom. This picture of life, blending past and present, suddenly unfolded an amazing *epiphany* and the revelation froze my entire being. *It seemed as if the wind had picked up the wisdom from the earth, and was whispering it into my heart.* I had just woken up after a brief nap on the bus ride and my mind was blank as if fresh and ready to receive…and the suggestion of the scene on the holy grounds was clear. Just two words of wisdom that reverberated with my years of research for the truth. The effect of the understanding jolted me and left me wide-eyed. As I experienced that suggestion, the truth of the prediction became clear. *The prediction of the "End of the World" was indeed true!*

I returned in bewilderment, interestingly again on an intriguing flight, 444 Air Mexico, and researched the realisation on arriving back home. All this was a little unnerving for me, considering my scientific background had always taught me to be skeptical and seek proof before believing anything. I felt a burning desire to investigate before sharing. And as the feeling of peace and tranquility in my own heart and life solidified with those two words, and the truth in that realisation synchronised with thousands of years of wisdom, there remained no doubt in my mind that it indeed was an genuine observation. Although I am neither a historian nor an authority in deciphering predictions, prophecies, or ancient texts, the last twenty-seven years as a physician and scientist had prepared me to analytically and logically reach a conclusion. Ironically, once the realisation sunk in, there was no need to think further, since it was replaced by a deep sense of knowing and understanding.

What is presented to you here is the result of that search and understanding, with a sincere hope that we all can realise what is coming and what is required of us...what part we need to fulfill to fit in...all for our own good.

The Mayan Temple in Chichen Itza.

Prologue

The world is 'after all a sum total of beings in a dynamic state of existence'. Among all the living entities, humans have been endowed with a unique central nervous system and physical body. This allows man to have the intellectual capability and physical capacity to make significant changes in his own lives as well as others. However, the attitude with which he perceives himself and others is the prime reason for his thoughts and actions. Therein, i.e., his observation of himself and others lies, the understanding that holds the key to knowing what the *End of the Word* truly means.

Tradition teaches us that there are three important events in our lives: Birth, Marriage and Death. But through all those, truly there is only one most important aspect that really matters and which is to find 'ourselves': our 'true identity'. Following Birth, we identify with a family of worldly origin. With Marriage, we ourselves create a new family. And with Death, we are released to yet another, possibly to the un-manifest family from where we came on earth to begin with.

We constantly perceive ourselves through the minds of family members, friends, community and colleagues. But then our image changes with different reflections by different people. So truly, *who are we*? And unless we know who we are, we cannot know our purpose on this earth, or how to live this life in a fulfilling and satisfying manner. The result is a world full of distress and chaos.

And yet each one of us is originally intended to live in a state of equilibrium and in a peaceful and joyous state. But that is not how the world's inhabitants' state is today. The world cannot continue in its current state and it has to end.

This realisation is not new, because the Mayans and many others in tune with "knowing the unforeseen" have predicted that the world in its current state will end.

What will replace it seems to elude us thus far, and yet that knowledge is essential to bring about what has been predicted.

Appeal to Readers

Truth does not need too many words. Once perceived, the simplest language of truth is indeed silence. However, since the history researched in this book spans thousands of years, as also the corelations made with applicable scientific knowledge, the details of the facts can be overwhelming. But it is not the intricacies of the factual details that are important. It is the discerning or the inference, which one gets while reading the information, which truly counts. Please hold on to that feeling, because therein lies the key to realisation of the truth. Some repetitions in the book are intentional to emphasise the importance of the subject matter. Some of the personal insights of the author are noted in *bold* print for easy review. Quotes by enlightened souls are also included.

Take your time to read what is to follow, but primarily, cultivate a familiarity with each sentence and you will perceive what is being referred to. This will come in the form of knowing in your heart, so there will be no need to use your own thoughts in the head to comprehend.

Enjoy your Journey and prepare to start living in bliss,

It is everyone's birth-right.

The Historic Playground at the Mayan Site.

Time and again signs are given to the perceivers. Whether they are perceived out of a 'small' individual mind or a 'big' universal mind is determined by the feeling it creates.

Feelings perceived by a 'small' individual mind are fear inducing and limiting. Those out of the 'big' universal mind are peaceful, uplifting, and expansive.

It is our choice what we want to identify with, believe in, and live as.

1

Mayan and Other Predictions

The Mayans were brilliant and highly insightful people who were very closely connected with Nature. They demonstrated a unique blend and deep understanding of both science and spirituality. Prior to the European conquest in central America, the Mayan civilisation flourished in regions including Honduras, Belize, Guatemala, and western El Salvador to as far away as central Mexico. Their civilisation prevailed in three phases: Pre-Classic (1500 BC to 3000 AD 300), Classic (AD 300 to 950), and Post-Classic (AD 950-1521, until arrival of Spanish).

Many of the Mayan texts were destroyed by the Spanish, possibly due to their dislike of some of the sacrificial practices or a need to establish their own supremacy. However, stories by the natives passed on through generations, and some surviving texts were left to tell their tale. Texts such as the *Dresden Codex* (named after the place where it was eventually lodged) shed light on some of the genius mathematical and astronomical models used by the Mayans. The information in those texts was used to understand the inscriptions on their constructs; hence, further insights into their beliefs and practices were obtained. Their reverence of the unseen power that creates and sustains the universe was obvious in rituals honouring it.

Similar to other Mesoamerican civilisations, Mayans developed many important aspects of human art and science. These included sculpture, architecture, written language, mathematics, and astronomy. They seemed to have specifically developed their expertise in counting time as days and years. One of their hallmarks towards keeping a tab on time was the development of the *"Mesoamerican Long Count Calendar"* along with their *Haab* (Solar) and *Tzolkin* (Sacred) calendars.

Their belief in the cyclical pattern of time led them to formulate the concept of *b'ak'tun,* or twenty *katun* cycles of the ancient Mayan Calender. This was equivalent to 144,000 days or 394.26 tropical years. Their *Mesoamerican Long Count* calendar dated back to 3,114 BC, therefore, their Classic Period fell in the eighth and nineth *b'ak'tun.* The current period following December 21, would fall in the 13th *b'ak'tun*. The way they read their *Long Count Calendar* included five digits separated by periods that read by the base number 20. The beginning of the cycle was read as 0.0.0.0.0 and referred to 11th August 3,114 BC.

Subsequently, each day was counted until day 20 and the end of 20 days was acknowledged as a month: 0.0.0.0.19 followed by 0.0.0.1.0 on day 20. Given this analogy the date December 21st, 2012 would be 13.0.0.0.0. Since the Mayans were superstitious about the number 13 and used it to describe the end of a cycle, this date received special attention.

Dr David Stuart of the University of Texas at Austin has extensively published on Mayan inscriptions records. He has stated that the only ancient monument that references the "end date" 13 *b'ak'tun* is the Monument six from Tortuguero, an archaeological site which Mayans inhabited in the Classic Period. Tortuguero is currently located in Tabasco, Mexico. Further elaboration on the Mayan decipherment is given by Stephen Houston, a renounceed epigrapher, who notes:

"In 1996, Stuart and I discussed part of the text on Tortuguero Monument six, suggesting that, on 13.0.0.0.0 4 Ajaw 3 K'ank'in, Julian December 10, AD 2012, a god will "descend," ye-ma or ye-mal, in what was held to be a nearly unique example of Classic-era prophecy......."

Grube Martin and Zender in their analytic report of the reading of Monument six have further noted the following:

"...the end of the 13th b'ak'tun which we will see in the year 2012" and as to what will happen, they say, "...utom, 'it will happen'..."

Mark Van Stone, Ph.D., with the Foundation for the Advancement of Mesoamerican Studies, Inc., who has closely followed the Mayan culture and history, concludes:

"... current debate about 21 December, 2012 results from contemporary confusion from projections, assumptions, and misunderstanding about the science and beliefs of several ancient cultures of the Americas."

The researchers of the phenomenon have recognised that the 13.0.0.0.0 Long Count dates suggest that the Mayans considered this phenomenon to be very unique. Its gigantic time spans and unusual alignment seem almost impossible to replicate in human history.

However, the Mayans were not necessarily expecting 2012 to be the end of the physical world. Their calculations refer to a *piktun* ending with a *piktun* of 20 *bak'tu'ns.* This could not happen if the *b'ak'tu'n* reset again after it reached 13. Hence, cataclysmic *or transformative events* could have been what they would foresee around December 21, 2012, which was considered as the end-date of a 5,125-year-long cycle in the *Mesoamerican Long Count* calendar.

It is not unexpected, then, that a large crowd gathered to witness the prediction of Mayan philosophy unfold and to commemorate the end of the *b'ak'tun* 13 on December 21, 2012, in the countries that were major parts of the Mayan civilisation. Such sites included cities in Mexico, Guatemala, Honduras, and El Salvador, with main events at Chichen Itza in Mexico and Tikal in Guatemala. Were these then the sites where unfolding of prophecy was to occur for a New World as the Mayans had marked that date as the end of a cycle?

Irrespective of what was intended, it appears that the Mayan prediction of the *'End of a Cycle'* somehow got distorted into the *'End of the World'* along the passage of time. But if we look closely, the word, 'World' truly means 'the state of existence of the earth's inhabitants'. However, in this case, two completely unconnected prophecies got entangled to produce a "breathtaking," "ultimate," and "all-important" perceived prophecy that shook the world!

This was the overhyped, *"End of the World"* story created by connecting the Mayan prediction with the foresight of the great seer and apothecary, Michel de Nostredame, also known as Nostradamus (AD 1503–1566). A well-known French medical healer, he paradoxically lost his first wife and a daughter to the plague and was devastated. He started having visions for the future, which he wrote in four-line (called quatrains) or six-line (simians) verses. He kept them intentionally vague to avoid persecution since they involved some intended prominent personalities and possibly catastrophic events. Among such predictions, some have been interpreted to represent the historic London Fire, the French Revolution, Napoleon's future, etc.

Nostradamus published collections of predictions that became famous world-wide. Among them is his book *Les Propheties*. Many of the prophecies deal with disasters, such as plagues, earthquakes, floods, droughts, battles, and wars. He stated that his prophecies extend to the year AD 3797. And yet, people have connected his 'perceived prophecies' with the announcement by Mayan's regarding their end of calendar cycle and concluded it as his *"End of World"* prediction date. The way this was publicised gave the impression that it was intended to mean physical demise of the world. It is remarkable how the world gets excited when someone adds two and two and makes it twenty two!

Going back to the question of the Mayan prediction, clearing it from any connection with Nostradamus, what were the Mayans referring to? Did the "end of…" refer to the Mayan world or mere turn of cyclic counting of days on the calendar? Or did it mean that the world will end existing in its current state and start evolving into another? Irrespective of what the Mayans were truly intending, many philosophers and scientists jumped on to the bandwagon of the possibility of the world coming to an end by various means. Predictions and hypothesis included torrential natural disasters resulting from: changes in polar-shift due to alignment between the galactic centre and Sun, or alterations in the earth's axis or strikes by asteroids or comets, etc. Although the perceived predictions by Mayans have been widely publicised and interpreted to create an erroneous fear of the future, such declarations in the field of eschatology are far too frequent to pay attention to all of them.

Oblivious to many, there have been more than fifty "predictions" pertaining to the limited existence of the world from individuals of many different faiths. Interestingly, all have different expiration dates for the world as a whole or in parts! These myths date back to the 6th millennium BC by the Romans, 3rd millennium by Hilary of Poitiers and Martin of Tours, Pope Sylvester II on January 1 1000, many European predictions for 1524, Jan Mathys Apocalypse in 1534, Martin Luther for 1600, Christopher Columbus in 1656-58, John Napier in 1700, Jean Dixon for 1962, Jehovah's witnesses for 1984, Louis Farrakhan that the Gulf War would be the War of Armageddon, Rollen Stewart and Lee Jang Rim for 1992, David Berg for 1993, Neal Chase for 1994, and many spiritual leaders for 2000 and 2012.

These absurd exercises have not yet ended, as such ridiculous and almost amusing calculations continue unabated for future possible dates predicting extinction! Jeane Dixon's date for 2020, Said Nursi's claim for 2129, Talmund's prediction for 2240...

Considering that Mother Earth continues to forge ahead with all her glory despite the increasing burden of human population, what do all the aforementioned dates indicate? Distractions? Warnings? *Or, are we to be careful when so-called "prophets" or "astrologers" distort genuine predictions and put images of gloom and doom? Could it be that some disturbed minds seek power and recognition and want to place negative outcomes in the minds of the masses so that their collective thinking can cause mass destruction? Have you noticed that all those who predicted "End of World", did so after their life-times were going to be over?*

The human race has to recognise that there is one principle in life that nature wants us to always keep in mind, whether it's the food we eat or the air we breathe or the company we keep:

If it does not FEEL good, peaceful and joyous, it is not right.

This is so because the perception by a limited and small human mind is prevailing over the expansive, big and universal mind.

Hence, before we accept any predictions, we have to analyse and 'feel' the statement. Since, the intelligent and perceptual Mayans never said anything about the physical destruction of the earth, what were they referring to? Could it be that there is more to these prophecies than what meets the eye?

Completely oblivious to so much history, our family walked on to the sacred site in Chichen Itza by a complete stroke of fate as if to witness the apocalypse (uncovering of the hidden knowledge) of that prediction! It is not possible for an alert and spiritually aware person to be in that environment and not have perceived it. But fate chose one with a scientific background and researching mind, seeking spiritual solace, to write about it. May be in the hope of bringing the understanding to the distressed world, a world that is completely enamoured by science, and has lost touch with their sixth sense, instinct, and insightful persona. In that state of existence the world seeks answers of the un-manifest by using logic and demanding proof!

.~.

Another Monument at the Mayan Site.

When we discover something wonderfully amazing, it is only natural to look at it from all directions and angles.

When that realisation pertains to the universe and it's creating and sustaining power, the search becomes even more compelling. Inquiry in such a matter has to date back to many realisations of the past leading up to the essence of the present; a sum total of revelations in different times and different places...

...when all sources point to the same knowledge, it has to be the truth...because truth transcends space and time...,and yet it may not be complete as time continues to unfold greater mysteries...

2

Universal Time Cycles

The Mayans' insight is commendable since they were able to perceive the future of the world without the knowledge and trend of world history. Independently, they were able to come to the same conclusion that had been unfolding through predictions for centuries before their civilisation blossomed and flourished. Before we look at what their prophecy was about, it is worth reviewing what the universe has been trying to disclose to us for thousands of years.

The universe is speculated to have existed for billions of years. While Earth and life on it has existed for millions of years, the oldest records of human existence as a fully developed, modern-behaviour man (*Homo-sapiens)*, has dated from 150,000 to 200,000 years ago. Historians suggest that older hominids (*a human like creature that stood upright*) may have prevailed for approximately 1.8 million years ago.

This is the time scale for us humans to consider. The spatial orientation is also mind-boggling...the Earth is a mere speck in the Universe, considering it is speculated to be 93 million miles from the sun and 165 quadrillion miles from the dark hole of the Milky Way. It itself is only about 8000 miles in diameter! Put this in perspective of the universe, which is thought to be probably about 80 octillion miles (80×10^{27}), each of us probably appears like a molecule of water in the spread of ocean! Who can be sure and who can prove it and how does it matter!

Irrespective of the time and spatial details of our external existence, the introspection of humans towards their true nature has been ongoing for a long time as well. Insights towards the paradigm of the internal and external world of mankind have emerged on earth at various times and different places. While man has feverishly sought answers about himself, given his realisation of a limited bodily existence on earth, he has also been fascinated, and yet, fearful of his enormous external world. Hence, humans have looked closely for signs of their own truth and of the truth outside of them. And just like he has been afraid of his own time cycle, he has questioned the existence of the world. Hence, many intelligent and insightful minds have deducted and left us with revelations and predictions.

It is difficult to say which of these are true revelations and predictions, but surely there is one important hallmark of *TRUTH.* And that is the following:

TRUTH transcends time and place,
because, it is constant and unchanging.

In the quest of the truth, therefore, it is only prudent to scale and analyse the realisations of information that has stood the test of time. As the wisdom of the past has been crystallised into present day texts, a careful study of these would reveal messages foretelling the *"End of World"* story. Let us look at some of these and their time-line.

There seems to be evidence that even in the earliest phase of human existence, even before written language had developed, ceramic carvings depicted man's realisation of a supernatural super-being; probably a realisation of an unmanifest power. As the story of mankind progressed, through Mesolithic and Neolithic Ages (Middle and New Stone Age) these realisations continued. And then, with the onset of the Agricultural Revolution, the nomadic existence of humans gave way to sedentary life and settlements, which gave a major impetus to human civilisation. As these civilisations grew more complex, thanks to the unique brain endowed to man, a system to record understandings and recommended practices led to the development of written texts.

Some the earliest (around 2500-2400 BC) of such written proofs pertaining to "supernatural affiliations" came from ancient Egypt in the form of the "Pyramid Text' and Sumerian religious accounts from Mesopotamia depicted in their cuneiform writings on clay tablets. Other prominent civilisations such as those in the Levant, (Jericho), Balkan Peninsula (Greece) and Indus Valley (Harappa) cultures showed signs of similar perceptions thousands of years ago.

.~.

The Levant and its site of Canaan (modern day Israel) are considered to be one of the oldest sites of origin of human civilisation. These showed similar revelations and understandings which date back to thousands of years. This knowledge was recorded in text as Holy (sacred, divine, and supernaturally revealed) Scriptures, the *Old Testament*, close to a thousand years before *Christ*. This book of knowledge has transcended three thousand years to tell its tale. Instrumental in the formation of this wisdom-laden book was a leader named Moses, who brought together Hebrew tribes during the Bronze Age. Although he was born to an Israelite family, fear of being killed prompted his mother to set him afloat on a river in a basket and be received by the Egyptian Pharaoh's family to be raised by them.

At a young age, he had to flee across the Red Sea after fighting injustice and eventually killing a slave master. On perceiving instructions from a higher power to lead his people to safety, he endured and led them out of Egypt. During that long journey, he received further instructions for humanity in the form of the *Ten Commandments*, which form a crucial part of the teachings of many faiths, including Judaism and Christianity. The foremost text, which is a compilation of various books reflecting life and teachings of those times, is the *Old Testament*. Mentioned in various books of the *Testament* are concerns of the *"End of the World"* and warnings associated with them.

Old Testament Bible:

Isaiah 13:6-7

"Wail, for the day of the LORD is near! It will come as destruction from the Almighty. Therefore, all hands will fall limp, and every man's heart will melt."

Joel 1:15

"Alas for the day! For the day of the LORD is near, and it will come as destruction from the Almighty."

~

If we study another region in the world, we see some highly intelligent understandings were scribed from the Indus Valley Civilisation (3000-1000 BC). These were noted as texts around 1500-1000 BC in the form of *Vedas* (meaning knowledge). They are a set of four scriptures: *Rig, Sama, Yajur, and Atharva*. Considered as adjuncts are some other crucial texts: the *Upanishads*, *Puranas*, and *Itihasas* such as *Ramayana* and *Mahabharata* (which have life stories of *Lord Rama* and *Krishna*). The *Mahabharata,* which is an extremely enlightening text to understand the duality and conflict of human existence today, is based on events leading to a major war held in Northern India in a place called Kurukshetra (Field of the King Kuru). In this battlefield, *Lord Krishna*, who is considered the personification of the Supreme Soul, speaks of human wisdom to a distressed warrior and devotee, Arjuna, in the midst of a major battlefield. In this war, Arjuna has to fight a very difficult situation of standing up against his own relatives for righteousness, *not unlike the "world war" we are living in today* (the war within ourselves because of our relationships and circumstances that prevents us from living in peace). This dialogue has culminated in one of the most venerated and essential texts in the form of the "*Bhagavad Gita*" (Song of God). Comprising eighteen chapters and about seven hundred total verses, the book gives a wealth of information and infinite wisdom to the readers including details of the human time cycles governed by the laws of the universe.

Pertaining to the aspect of eschatology (combination of theology, philosophy, astrophysics, etc., dealing with the future), the *Bhagavad Gita* refers to the human existence on Earth in time cycles designated as *"kalpas"* in Sanskrit language. The symbolic *"End of the World"* gets referred to as cyclical human existence as follows:

Bhagavad Gita

Chapter 9: 7

"All beings take on my (Creator of Universe), nature when an age ends, son of Kunti (referring to Arjuna, the disciple, who is receiving knowledge). I (Supreme Soul), project them again when the new age begins."

The cyclical nature of human existence is explained in detail to go through stages or periods of human transformation during each cycle. As per ancient Hindu scriptures, these are referred to as "*yugas*". This is further expanded in that holy text as follows:

Bhagavad Gita:

Chapter 8:17

"Those who know that the day of Brahma consists of a thousand yugas, the night of Brahma comprising a thousand yugas, those people know day and night."

How many "*yugas*" are there in one "*kalpa*" is elaborated in a related ancient text called the *Srimad Bhagwatam (Book of God) from the same period.* This text delineates the four "*yugas*" as follows:

Satya yuga (Golden Period)- the period of truth, virtue and wisdom;

Treta yuga (Silver Period)- the period of introduction of vice;

Dvapara yuga- (Copper Period)- the period of increasing vice;

Kali yuga (Iron Period)- the period of predominant vice.

These "*yugas*" or periods of time cycles recur in cyclical pattern in ascending, then descending phases.

Srîmad Bhâgavatam

3.11.18

"Maitreya (Enlightened friend) said: O Vidura, the four millenniums are called the Satya, Tretâ, Dvâpara and Kali yugas. The aggregate number of years of all of these combined is equal to twelve thousand years of the demi-gods".

The cyclical time periods start with the golden and end with the iron phases sequentially. When last period of predominant vice or "*Kali yuga*" peaks it brings in the end of that period with the rectification by enlightened souls to eventually reintroduce the "*Satya" yuga* (period of truth, virtue and wisdom). This occurs after the cyclical return of each of the other *yugas* through the paths of ascending *Dvapara* (period of more vice, less virtue and wisdom), *Treta* (period of less vice, more virtue and wisdom), and finally *Satya* (period of truth, virtue and wisdom). This collection further elaborates the possible duration of each of these cycles. According to it the total duration of such a cycle is about 12,000 "demi-god" years. It suggests that one "demi-god" year is about 360 human years!

Srîmad Bhâgavatam

3.11.19

"The duration of the Satya millennium equals 4,800 years of the years of the demi-gods; the duration of the Dvâpara millennium

equals 2,400 years; and that of the Kali millennium is 1,200 years of the demi-gods."

Hence, it becomes apparent that a cyclic nature of the universal time cycles was perceived by ancient enlightened humans as early as many thousand years ago. However, in those realisations they attributed it to the changing trends in human realisation and conceptual living state.

.~.

The year 563 BC, saw the arrival on earth of an amazing enlightened being, born as a handsome prince. Heir to a kingdom in Lumbini (located in ancient India, modern day Nepal), he grew up amid highly desirous lifestyle. He was conceived after twenty years of marriage by what is considered to be a divine intervention. But much to the grief of the family, his mother died seven days after his birth. At the age of twenty-nine, this prince, Siddhartha Gautama, felt distressed despite all the riches afforded to a prince, including a beautiful and loving wife and a wonderful son, kingdom, and fame. He felt the need to search for the higher truth, to seek happiness, as he realised that everything he had materialistically was impermanent. This realisation came to him as he witnessed the distress caused by death, disease, and old age, when he stepped outside the walls of his protected castle. Leaving all materialistic possessions, his family, and kingdom, he went to the forest to meditate and seek the answers to end the root cause of human sorrow.

After six years of seeking wisdom, Buddha emerged enlightened, having achieved "*Nirvana*" (realisation that liberated him from suffering) and started teaching the path to true self and happiness. Through his understanding, he offered the experience of the Four Immeasurable: love, compassion, joy, and equanimity. He lived in peace teaching until the end of his life at age of eighty. His original teachings were recorded in the sacred scriptures, 'Canon *Tripitaka*' (three baskets: *Vinaya, Sutta,* and *Abhidhamma Pitakas)* and were practised in South Asia as Theravada Buddhism with the human's life purpose to become *"Arhat"* or "enlightened". Subsequently, more scriptures and teachings and rituals were added as the practice spread to the Northern Asia and is referred to as Mahayana Buddhism. Even the insightful Buddha perceived the *"End of the World"*.

Sutta Pitaka:

Buddha said,

"After my decease, first will occur, the five disappearances. And what are the five disappearances?" The disappearance of attainments [to nibbana], the disappearance of the method [inability to practise wisdom, insight and the four purities of moral habit], the disappearance of learning [loss of men who follow the Dhamma and the forgetting of the Pitakas and other scriptures], the disappearance of the symbols [the loss of the outward forms, the robes and practices of monkhood], the disappearance of the relics [the Dhatu]..."

"Then when the Dispensation of the perfect Buddha is 5000 years old, the relics, not receiving reverence and honour will go to places where they can receive them... This, Sariputta, is called the disappearance of relics."

~

Fast forward the times to the next major event in the history of mankind that changed the way man has perceived his origin and the mystic future: the arrival of *Jesus Christ* on earth. After undertaking only three years of teaching and healing in Israel, it became apparent that he was a supernatural phenomenon, as had been predicted at the time of his birth. Before he undertook this wonderful life of preaching and healing, he observed fast and prayed for forty days in the wilderness. There, his communion with the Supreme Power, referred to by many as God, led him to have amazing insights and wisdom of self and the right way to live life.

Endowed with supernatural healing powers, close to the age of thrity years, he went about teaching and healing in towns and cities of

Israel. He was aware that what he was about to reveal to the world would be "unbelievable" for many non-believers, so he took with him twelve selected men, referred to as the Apostles, who would live to tell the story and take his teachings forward in time and spread them in far off regions. As he appeared to his followers even on the third day after his crucifixion, death, and burial, the powers of the unseen force, could not be denied by those who witnessed it. It took more than three hundred years after his death to compile all his teachings, which were collected through his disciples' accounts and passed on through generations. The final account, the *New Testament* of the *Holy Bible*, is one the most revered scriptures as well as one of the most commonly read texts world-wide. Even in that holy book, a mention of significant changes in our existence has been foretold.

New Testament Bible:

Luke 21:25-26

"And there will be signs in sun and moon and stars, and on the earth distress of nations in perplexity because of the roaring of the sea and the waves, people fainting with fear and with foreboding of what is coming on the world. For the powers of the heavens will be shaken."

Matthew 24:21-22:21

"For then there will be great distress, unequalled from the beginning of the world until now—and never to be equalled again. If those days had not been cut short, no one would survive, but for the sake of the elect those days will be shortened."

Mark 13:8

"For nation will rise against nation, and kingdom against kingdom. And there will be earthquakes in various places, and there will be famines and troubles. These are the beginnings of sorrows."

.~.

Another event in history that marks the revelations of "messages" from powers higher than common human perception occurred between AD 570 and 632 in the Arabian Peninsula. Prophet Muhammad Rasul Allah, perceived words from the Supreme Power by his higher-self while meditating and praying in caves; thence emerged the Islamic scriptures. This was despite a very heart-wrenching childhood wherein he lost both his parents by the age of seven.

He was born in Mecca and before his birth; his father fell ill on a business journey and died. Interestingly, the Prophet came from the ancestors belonging to "Ismail" also referred to as "Ishmael", who was the son of "Ibrahim" also called "Abraham" (The same lineage from which Judaism and Christianity originated). His mother had a dream that her son was going to bring light to the world and should be named Ahmad.

She faced hardships as she raised him and passed away by the time he was six to seven years old. His neighbours transported him to his grandfather, who took over his care and changed his name to Muhammad and had him learn animal husbandry. But at the age of eight in AD 578, he was given to his uncle (Abu Talib) as his grandfather died. Thereafter, he was raised by his uncle and protected and provided for by him.

Known from a young age to be truthful and sincere, Muhammad is said to have received the attention of a Christian monk, Baheera, on one of his trips with his uncle. Baheera noticed the child's bright face and predicted he would do great things. His sincerity and honesty earned him the title of Al Amin (Honest One) in his teenage period. At the age of twenty-five, he married a business woman and worked hard to help them flourish. In his influential position, he worked to eradicate slavery in Mecca.

He started spending increasing time in prayers and meditation, which he undertook in a cave called Hira. Over the next twenty-three years, one hundred and fourteen chapters of the *Holy Qur'an* were put together. This scripture again sheds light on that possibility of the *"End of the World"*.

Qur'an:

AlHijr; [15:85]

"We did not create the heavens and the earth, and everything between them, except for a specific purpose. The end of the world will come, so treat them with benign neglect".

AlKahf: [18:21]

"We caused them to be discovered, to let everyone know that God's promise is true, and to remove all doubt concerning the end of the world. The people then disputed among themselves regarding them. Some said, "Let us build a building around them." Their Lord is the best knower about them. Those who prevailed said, "We will build a place of worship around them."

Turning over another thousand years in history, one of the most peaceful, loving, and spiritually evolved Souls to have walked on the earth in recent times is Guru Nanak Devji (AD 1469-1539), (*Guru* means Spiritual Master). Born into a Hindu family near Lahore, which was originally Indian territory but now a part of Pakistan post-independence of 1947, he was marked by predictions to represent a highly placed saint. Even as a child, he amazed people around him with utterances full of deep wisdom and mystical occurrences and revelations. He grew up during the times when India was occupied and ruled by the Mogul Empire (Muslims); hence, both Hindu and Islamic saints influenced the society. One of his most amazing replies as a child was a response to a query as to why he was reciting both Hindu and Islamic scriptures, and he said, "God is neither Hindu nor Muslim". His followers after his passing away established the Sikh religion and recorded *Gurubani* (Word of God) in respected Sikh scriptures, mainly the *Sri Guru Granth Sahib*. Composed of 5894 hymns full of loving praise for God, compiled by *Guru* Arjun Devji, the most amazing aspect of this wonderful scripture is that it not only contains true and deep wisdom of the Sikh *Gurus*, but it also includes teachings from Hindu and Muslim saints. Interestingly, even this Holy Scripture perceives the concept of *"End of the World"*.

Sri Guru Granth Sahib:

Page 1100

"The earth, the Akaashic ethers of the sky, the nether regions of the underworld, the moon and the sun shall pass away. Emperors, bankers, rulers and leaders shall depart, and their homes shall be demolished.

The poor and the rich, the humble and the intoxicated, all these people shall pass away. The qazis, sheikhs and preachers shall all arise and depart.

The spiritual teachers, prophets and disciples—none of these shall remain permanently. Fasts, calls to prayer and sacred scriptures—without understanding, all these shall vanish.

The 8.4 million species of beings of the earth shall all continue coming and going in reincarnation. The One True Lord God is eternal and unchanging. The Lord's slave is also eternal."

Page 1204

"The mountains, the earth, the water and the air shall pass away. Only the Word of the Holy Saint shall endure. Those born of eggs shall pass away, and those born of the womb shall pass away. Those born of the earth and sweat shall pass away as well.

The four Vedas shall pass away, and the six Shastras shall pass away. Only the Word of the Holy Saint is eternal".

There are many more predictions voicing the same concern: *"End of the World":* reverberating like ripples created by one stone in the ocean of mankind's history. But the one that got the most attention was undoubtedly *the Mayan prediction*. However, the question remains: what is the truth behind all these predictions?

.~.

Vibrant Skies Blessing the Mayan Site.

The truth of a revelation lies in its depth of perception. The only way to truly appreciate a new realisation is to sit with it without any thoughts of your own, as if receiving it with an empty or new mind.

It comes then as an understanding that is beyond words, unadulterated by any internal dialogue. Only in this fresh state of mind can the unfolding and flowering of a truthful realisation occur. It is the only rescue we have left in the world of insanity today, and the future of the universe begs it of us.

3

True Meaning of the 'Predictions'

What have all these predictions been alluding to when they talk about the *"End of the World"?* Considering that the much publicised prediction of the "doomsday" has become history without physical destruction of the world, might it be that there is a metamorphic intent behind those predictions? And indeed if we look at the origin and interpretation of the word "world," it refers to the "earthly state of human existence". Hence, the questions which arise out of this issue would have to be:

1. What is the world now?
2. What is that which needs to end?
3. How will that come to be?
4. What will it result in?

The world that we exist in today has grown exponentially in number and complexity in the last few hundred years. It has been reported that approximately twenty times increase has occurred in the world population in the last 600 years. The rates of crimes including homicides involving innocent people extending to small children in schools is appalling, to say the least. Mental and psychosomatic illnesses including depression, anxiety, and suicide and physical disorders such as hypertension, diabetes and cancer are at an unexpected high. Additionally, there are an increasing number of individuals falling prey to addictions. No social or economic class is exempt from such a curse. It appears that we are living in the '*Kali Yuga*' (period of disorder with predominant vice and untruth) referred to in Chapter 2, that has been described in ancient texts from almost five thousand years ago.

- *but why is the world full of disorder, distress and disease?*
- *and where is all this chaos in the world leading to?*

The answers may appear complex but are truly very simple and reveal in the following wisdom:

It is a most unfortunate aspect of our lives today that we carry a very restrictive and, in some ways, distorted view of ourselves.

When we live out of this distorted view, we are only going to lead a distorted life.

A distorted life will bring in disorder, distress and disease.

This philosophy of seeing ourselves in a limited scope yields to us only a fraction of our true self and potential. This partially-perceived image frustrates and stifles our existence and compels us to undertake short-cut measures that are often against the universal laws of creation, empowerment, synchrony, and sustenance. When such practice becomes widespread, as it is today, the result is world of complete chaos, dishonesty, mistrust, selfishness, evil intent, distress, destruction, and headed towards ultimate dissolution. Dissolution—because the extent of distress will be so overwhelming that it will culminate in unhappy people all over engaging in widespread offensive acts towards themselves and others.

The degree of distress and insanity of the human mind has crossed all unthinkable limits today, when even innocent children are not being spared from acts of sexual abuse and deadly violence.

This is only a display of the extreme distress, hate, and complete lack of self-control. How can we allow such a tragic outcome of disturbed minds? How come there is no responsibility shown by the minds that conduct it and those who allow it? The current unacceptable state of anger, fear-filled, conceited, and mistrusting existence of human minds urgently requires us to question our perplexing state and implement equally urgent corrective measures. Might there be a simple explanation and cure for this distress? It may indeed be. Given our complex and unnecessarily involved lives today, we do not have time to understand, who we truly are and hence do not know how to conduct ourselves.

With an incomplete and erroneous understanding of self, we cannot expect to live a complete and correct life.

The hidden, unseen and unmanifest aspect of ourselves beckons us in a different direction of an amazing world of order and peace, if only we can pause to understand it for our own profit.

Only by this complete understanding about self, can we have a happy, contented and fulfilling life.

And when we all are living out of such an understanding, then the world can exist in a state that it was intended to be in, peaceful and joyful.

That is the New World which is about to emerge, and we all have to do our part.

And it starts with a simple understanding of our complete identity and true higher self.

But what is our complete identity and what is our true higher self? We often have just enough time to get a glimpse of ourselves in the mirror now and then. That gives us our physical image. Then we run around all over interacting with others either in person or phone or cyber space or putting ourselves at the mercy of the radio or television and subjecting ourselves to electronic abuse and feel that we know ourselves mentally. In fact, what we are looking at is a reflection of the outer world in ourselves: *Our distorted view is the reflection in the mirror, eyes, and minds of others.* This so-called understanding gives us our physical and mental image of self, which most people in today's world feel is our complete identity.

The truth is that this physical and mental image of self is not our true identity. These are mere coverings of an inner wondrous and exquisite core that we all possess, obscured by an untrained mind, which has only been trained to look outside us. Our true identity is, in fact *THE LIFE FORCE* responsible for our being alive. This life force is within us, and what a paradox that we seek our self by looking outside. It is only after a complete understanding of this Life Force can we comprehend the true meaning of the predictions alluding to *"End of the World"*.

.~.

To proceed with obtaining a clear recognition of our true self, please take a few moments to ponder over the following questions:

How often do we sit still, quiet, or in solitude without thoughts of how others perceive us or interact with us to get a peek at our true identity? And yet, it is the *most important realisation* we need to have; otherwise, we are completely at the mercy of everyone else to determine who we are! And at the last counting, there are about seven billion people in the world to give you all kinds of opinions!

Is this not insanity? How can what other people say, or think, help us determine what we truly are? How can we allow ourselves to be at the mercy of what others say, or how they act to make us feel any different? Why should another's words and actions interfere with our peace of mind? Why would a feeling that we are lower than "expected" make us feel miserable and tormented? By what standards are these expectations set anyways? If everyone's thoughts, words and actions are continuously changing due to the dynamic nature of the world, then are we ever going to be at peace? What a sorry situation that we keep polishing the image in the mirror, refining it and defining ourselves by it. The true identity of a person is not even recognised. What we keep focussing on is the outer manifestation of our existence: our physique (body) and our personality (mind). Only a few get a glimpse of the truthful, peaceful, and pure identity; our soul. This true identity can be perceived in our character. It is our core energy. It is the life force within us. Its inherent nature is peaceful and joyful. It intends to exist in *sync*: within and without, united with the energy all around us and with the power that created it. In that state it finds bliss. Since most of us are so preoccupied with our body and mind, we have no clue about this entity, energy, force... No wonder, considering that we are living in a distorted image of ourselves, indeed this is only going to produce a distorted life.

This disparity has become so common that it is considered a norm, and people are often heard questioning the entity of the soul! Despite multiple revelations in history by prominent "Soul-conscious" humans that have left their footprints as scriptures, doubts are created by "so-called scientific minds" about these epiphanies. Although, 85 per cent of the world population follows some form of religion, many scoff at the identity of a soul and higher power, demanding scientific proof.

It is prudent that we critically understand one thing for our own good:

Science may have done many wonders, but it has not created this universe. Nor has any human or scientific process created life.

Science only *discovers* what nature has created and *utilises and improvises*. The natural phenomenon and it marvels at the amazing powers of the nature! Furthermore, even science is beginning to realise a power within all of us that remains unseen but can be experienced. Many such claims of realisation date back to thousands of years. Recent works of many physicians and scientists such as Dr Brian Weiss (Professor of Psychiatry and author of *Many Lives, Many Masters* and *Same Soul Many Bodies*) and Dr Jeffery Long (Director of Near Death Experience Research Foundation) have demonstrated the truth of this life force entity in their own research. My own father's experience of encountering blissful light in a near death event and a couple of my own experiences wherein I have encountered supernatural power in deep meditative states as well flashes of seeing the future have left me with no doubt about this truth. This has been substantiated in experiences of many other people revealing the reality of a life force, an energy within us that is only evident with deep insight in a state where ordinary mind, which blocks it's realisation, is transcended.

Despite a plethora of evidence to support this realisation, many are skeptical and do not whole-heartedly believe this truth. But it is indeed amazing that even though we cannot see molecules of oxygen, carbon dioxide and nitrogen hovering around in air, we accept the explanations by chemists that these are present in the atmosphere. Why does our mind not question such an *ideation* of molecules and atoms, even when we cannot see them? On the other hand, why does our mind does not want to dwell more upon the soul entity present in each one of us? The reason is simple: nothing threatens the survival or supremacy or be-all entity of the mind than the realisation of the soul. By accepting the presence of this hidden aspect of our identity, the mind loses its perceived rule over the "kingdom" of self. But this "mind ruler" is very limited, whimsical, and at the mercy of the external world and will never let any of us exist in peace or perpetual joy. Hence, it is to our own best advantage to at least attempt to seek this reality. It would be a shame if we complete a life-time cycle and do not know ourselves completely.

How can we leave this earth without knowing ourselves fully!

If there is more to us, why not get acquainted with it before we spend more time with others and subject ourselves to increasing confusion and torture!

In a body-conscious state, we seek pleasures associated with the body. Often these are so compelling that we give no consideration to norms or values that will ensure equilibrium. The mind-conscious image dictates us to pursue coveted positions, power, riches, fame and impressive personality traits often without developing our character or respecting the feeling and needs of others. However, by nature, the body changes and decays over time since it is, after all, merely a matter. The vicious cycle of disease, old age, and death are inevitable. Mind, similarly, is never steady and swings to extremes, often dictated by rapidly changing emotions of pleasure, sadness, fear, anger, acceptance, and disgust and is impossible to keep steady. As our external interactions, situations, body form, professional undertakings, economic stability, and relationships alter, so does our internal state, if we are body-conscious or mind-conscious. As our state of mind gets disturbed and tormented by what the *mind perceives as 'unacceptable,'* each change in our physical state, relationship, or circumstance sets our body and mind-conscious entity in a roller-coaster-like, perpetually reactive existence. This unsteadiness brings with it restlessness and distress, often culminating in anxiety and depression. It is sad that one can pass an entire lifetime tormented and tossing in despair, when with one simple realisation we can have a completely different life of complete peace and joy!

Hence, man is tossing and turning under the dictatorship of the body and mind when originally he was intended to be a pure, peaceful soul, embodied in the body to experience, create, synchronise, and enjoy in this world.

For the soul to enjoy and participate in the material world, it had to be placed in a material body, and the mind was needed to help the soul operate the body.

However, over time and with self and world induced stresses, the mind got so overused that the soul was completely overshadowed and hidden.

And unfortunately, the mind became way too powerful and took over with its own agenda, and chaos ensued. This is not unlike a car (body) being driven by a cruise control engine (mind) wherein the driver (soul) has been put to sleep and is not allowed to operate by an overwhelmingly controlling cruise control. Unfortunately, the mind (cruise control engine) is bound to eventually crash the system unless the soul (driver) takes over and starts operating with guided principles, giving due respect to fellow cars and drivers.

In essence, what has gone wrong in our existence as a human race is that we have become an increasingly body and mind-conscious society and have completely overlooked our soul-conscious identity?

True happiness is only possible when we return to our original state of being soul-conscious.

•~•

Now, let us look into the question: *What if we become soul-conscious beings?*

Na jayate mriyate va kadacin nayam bhutva bhavita va na Bhuyah ajo nityah sasvato yam purano na hanyate hanyamane sarire.

"For the soul there is neither birth nor death at any time. He has not come into being, does not come into being, and will not come into being. He is unborn, eternal, ever-existing and primeval. He is not slain when the body is slain."

Knowing that our soul is energy force, unchanging, capable of neither death nor destruction, the changes and demands of the body and mind do not have the potential to dismay us anymore.

Suddenly we realise that there is truly no need to distress over anything! In that state of realisation, we are suddenly full of peace and can truly experience joy. Can you imagine a world full of peaceful and joyous people? What a wonderful world will that be!

It was the search of this very realisation that drove Buddha away from all the riches and comforts of materialistic life even when he had access to luring fame and power. He recognised that old age, disability, disease, and death were inevitable. He realised that these were associated with dismay, distress and mourning.

But amongst all this, he noticed a peaceful saint who sat undisturbed. He knew intuitively that there was more to him than the physically and mentally perceived manifested existence, and he set out to find out the higher truth...If Buddha could search and find that higher truth and through it invincible peace and joy, why would it not be possible for all of us? And can that happen while we are still in our materialistic world, in the midst of our professional and family lives? The answer is *YES;* we can find our entire truth and complete entity and the higher truth-our core life force, wherein is the wisdom, peace, and joy that can transform our lives to one of bliss. If I can perceive it, anyone can..*RIGHT HERE AND RIGHT NOW!* Are *YOU* ready? The realisation of our higher self can occur in a fraction of a second, and the perception will change us forever...for the better...to help us lead the best life possible for each of us.

It is this awareness that can transform our disturbed lives to one of infinite and eternal bliss. With that change the prediction of "the end of the world...in its current form" will be fulfilled as each one of us reaches that awareness.

Hence, there will be an end to the existence of the world struggling with vice, strife, distress, and mistrust and will be replaced by a world full of peace, joy, wisdom, and success!

And the texts that have survived thousands of years, tell the same truth.

.~.

In Chapter 3, Additional Universal Wisdom

Old Testament:

Genesis 2:7

"Then the Lord God formed the man of dust from the ground and breathed into his nostrils the breath of life, and the man became a living soul".

Ecclesiastes 12:7

"And the dust returns to the earth as it was, and the spirit returns to God who gave it."

Bhagavad Gita:

Chapter 2: 17, 20

"Know that which pervades the entire Body is indestructible. No one is able to destroy the imperishable soul.

For the soul there is neither birth nor death.

Nor, having once been, does he ever cease to be. He is unborn, eternal, ever-existing, undying and primeval. He is not slain when the Body is slain.

New Testament Bible:

Matthew 10:28

"And do not fear those who kill the Body but cannot kill the Soul. Rather fear him who can destroy both Soul and Body in hell."

Matthew 16:26:

"For what is a man profited, if he shall gain the whole world, and lose his own Soul."

Qur'an:

Surat Al-Hijr [15:29]

"So when I have made him complete and breathed into him of my spirit (ruh), fall down making obeisance to him".

Surat Qâf **(50:21)**

"And every Soul comes, with it a driver and a witness.

Guru Granth Sahib:

Page 421

"Those who understand their own souls are themselves the Supreme Soul."

Page 441

"O my Self ! you are of the nature of light; do recognise your origin."

.~.

Ruins Along a Large Majestic Well in Chichen Itza.

Immortality attracts humans because we view ourselves as mortal creatures. In this state of perceived mortal existence we try hard to be noticed, appreciated, and accepted and often live in fear and anxiety of past and future.

However, a simple realisation frees us of the pain and burden of proving ourselves again and again, or tossing between despair and distress.

Once that realisation infiltrates our core, it begins to resound in our being. We start existing in complete peace and joy...without the need of another person's approval or change in circumstances...

And guided by our innate wisdom we start living in bliss with unconditional love and respect.

4

One Death for Eternal Life of Bliss

In the beginning of summer of 2012, we attended a very touching funeral service of a colleague's daughter. Unfortunately, she had breathed her last from an infection when she was hardly 25 years old. Her relatives and close friends paid glowing tributes to her, filled with overflowing display of love and affection. I was so moved that the following month, I celebrated my own fiftieth birthday with about fifty close friends and relatives in a restaurant *as my own funeral*. As we enjoyed dinner and drinks, laughing and engaging in conversation, I suddenly announced that I wanted all those who had collected to pretend I was dead. As if they were at my funeral, I wanted them to let me know what they would want to say about me at my funeral. In that paradoxical celebration, I truly felt completely liberated and free. Since, I did not need to worry or be concerned about anything, I felt complete peaceful within. Each moment was filled with a sense of deep enjoyment and I felt an upsurge of love flow out from my core and throughout the room!

Glowing tributes from all my friends and family members ensued as they were amazingly accepting of me. Their conversations were only about the unconditional love we had shared in our relationships. After all, the speakers had unfolded their heartfelt feelings, I let them know my own positive perceptions of their presence in my life. It was an amazingly powerful, and yet humbling, *albeit* peaceful and joyous experience.

However, it was ironic that in my "alive" state, none of them had communicated such feelings to me. The most perplexing realisation was this: how can someone be so appreciated and loved when one is "dead" and never have such feelings expressed during the period when one is "alive"! And how can one feel so peaceful and joyous when one is supposed to be "dead." What "died" that evening for all of us to feel so wonderful about each other? Before we answer that crucial question, let us examine what we know.

It is said that the eyes cannot see what the mind does not know. Probably, the reverse is also true in that the mind does not tend to believe in what the physical body cannot sense. And yet, the greatest powers of creation and sustenance are unseen and not physically manifest!

And that unseen, all powerful, unmanifest energy is the soul within each of us and the Universal Energy and Power outside us.

It is through this Universal Energy and Power that our soul derives its energy to be alive.

Scientists tell us that all matter is composed of molecules that are in motion and these are further made up of atoms, each of which has protons, neutrons, and electrons. They further elaborate that the electrons are in motion around a central nucleus of neutrons and protons, not unlike what they tell us about the planets running in paths around the Sun. We cannot physically see any of these atoms, electrons, neutrons, protons, and still we have no objections in accepting it as *truth*. And yet, when someone who has experienced the presence of his soul tells us about it, we raise our eyebrows and question that fact. Isn't it amazing that we have so much knowledge of things outside us and don't even know ourselves fully when all our lives we live with ourselves!

~

The cynic mind is quick to question: "But if we all have a soul, how come only some experience it?" Can all of us experience it? A simple and truthful answer is in the affirmative! And a simple comprehension can reveal this simple yet profound truth. For that to happen you will have to see yourself as an onion. You have to patiently "peel your layers" or rather "feel your layers" to completely and fully realise yourself. The first layer is your physical body, comprised about a hundred trillion cells (10^{14}) organised into eleven organ systems listed below:

1. Skin,
2. Skeletal,
3. Muscular,
4. Digestive,
5. Circulatory,
6. Respiratory,
7. Endocrine,
8. Nervous,
9. Urinary,
10. Reproductive,
11. Lymphatic.

The next peel is our mental entity, which itself is a multi-layer, semi-hidden attribute in that. Although we know what is going on in our minds, no one can really 'see' the activity. Anatomically, the main seat of our mental activity is in the brain. For the sake of simplicity the brain can be divided structurally into three important parts:

1. The *top* portion of the brain (cerebral cortex): The seat of intellectual thoughts such as reading, comprehension, mathematic computation, etc.
2. The *mid* portion of the brain (hippocampus): The region associated with feelings, such as fear, anger, happiness, sadness, disgust, acceptance, and surprise.
3. The *lower* portion of the brain (pons and medulla): The area that is able to help us experience the physical world around us

by its connections with the sense organs (sight, smell, hearing, taste, touch) and with the higher centres (parietal, occipital, and temporal lobes); in this part also lie the centres for regulating breathing and heart-beat, which run autonomically although influenced by various nervous centres and chemicals in the body.

The above details are the *structural* format where the mind resides. However, more importantly, it is crucial to understand the *functional* aspect of the mental entity because in it resides the path to realisation and liberation from despair.

Only with this comprehensive overview and knowledge can we appreciate the true meaning of the predictions concerning "End of the World".

.~.

Conceptually, the functional aspect of our mental make-up can be perceived as the intelligent, emotional mind, and observational mind. These are the conscious manifestation of its function. There is another aspect, which is the sub-conscious mind that manifests itself as dreams during sleep. And yet another, and probably the most important, aspect of the mind is the super-consciousness, which is pure awareness. This is the state of *realisation* when all activities of the mind are on stand-still in the awaken state.

It is in that state of awareness—still mind with super-conscious alertness—that we perceive our Soul.

It sounds simple, but why do most of us have such a difficult time understanding and experiencing this simple truth? The reason is an over-active and often dysfunctional, emotional mind that our human race has developed due to repeatedly inflicting on ourselves self-created, unnecessary mental stresses. This emotionally active mind keeps us in a constant state of distress and distracts all our attention to itself. But the fact remains that we are way more than our emotional, ego-driven mind. In fact, we are a combo deal; just like we get a drink, main course, and dessert for our meal, we come packaged as:

Body, Mind, and Soul.

Irrespective of how we perceive our layers, one fact even science cannot deny. All aspects of our existence is, after all, merely a manifestation of physical, chemical and electrical symphony! A figurative way of understanding this concept is to look at ourselves as lamps. The physical structure of the lamp is the body. Just like a lamp can have different shapes, heights, colours, we all differ in our outer aspect. The body shows itself as physique.

The bulbs placed in the lamp symbolise the mind, which again can differ in their voltage. Therefore, different individuals have different degrees of mental traits, often referred to as intelligence and personality. One lamp may have brighter light than another just as one person may appear more intelligent than another.

But neither the lamp nor the bulbs will have any shine or use if there is no electric current running through them. This current is the spirit and the *irradiance* is the soul, which illuminates everything in our being. To receive the current, we have to be plugged in or connected to a source of energy. Once created, life is self-perpetuating, but the existence of unlimited resources, longevity, brilliance, and limitless potentials are only possible if we are connected to solar power or a continuously generating power-house. Otherwise, using local batteries, generators, etc., will result in easy burn out. This super power-house of energy is the Universal Power, what many refer to as the Supreme Power, Higher Power, Almighty, or God. Through the energy dissipated by the Universal Power, our own soul energy gets recharged continuously.

The important aspect of this comparison is to realise that even though the lamp may break or the bulbs may fuse, but the current will always be there in one form or another. That immortal identity of ours is true for all of us. And since we all come from the same source, which is the powers of the universe, the inter-connections among all of us cannot be ignored. Symbolically, we can see ourselves as the rays of Sun, all radiating from the same source of energy and light. This understanding has been around for thousands of years and has been tapped into by many famous people as well as saints, who have had access to this information through ancient scriptures or teachings of their spiritual masters. Like a sacred secret and key to liberation it has been handed down to those who have sought it. I feel that if there is something wonderful and life-transforming that can end the suffering of everyone, this should be discussed with all humans.

Because living in peace and bliss is not a chance phenomenon, it is our birth right.

.~.

An analogy to clarify the concept of body, mind, and soul is to look at a human as a car (body), engine (mind), and driver (soul). The driver (soul) needs the car (body) to get around in this world. To operate the car (body), the driver (soul) needs the engine (mind). There are four apparent usual-use gears in the engine (mind). Sub and super-conscious minds are as follows:

P = Parking = Observational Mind,

R = Reverse = Memory for Intelligent Mind,

N = Neutral = Free-floating thoughts- Emotional Mind,

D = Drive = Intelligent Mind,

D-2 = Drive on Higher Altitude = Super-conscious Mind,

Key out, engine off = Sub-conscious Mind.

As we all know, if the car is left in neutral, it can go just about anywhere depending on the circumstance, slope, etc. Similarly, if we leave the mind in the zone of the ego-driven, emotional mind, we can land up any and everywhere! Chaos, accidents, and eventual tragedies are bound to happen in that state of existence. Therefore, an unintelligent existence leaves us at the mercy of the havoc played out by this part of the mind, which is most of the time "*out of control.*" The greatest attribute of this overactive emotional mind is that it is constantly obsessed with thoughts related to "I" or "me."

In that state of frenzy, controlled by the ego, our own minds keep us locked into THOUGHTS from the past and future pertaining to our relationships, circumstances, or self-created image.

The most compelling attribute of this frenzy is non-acceptance at some level.

By simply realising that our true self is the soul, which has capability to connect with the universe, we find ourselves complete and acceptable irrespective of our relationships or circumstances.

In that instant of acceptance our mind stops whining and the present moment becomes alive, as the observational and intelligent mind is no more over-ridden by the dysfunctional ego mind.

The amazing understanding then dawns on us that all these disturbing feelings are caused by,

Merely Thoughts; None of it is the Truth Now Because the Only Truth is the Present Moment!

The easiest way to realise what this overactive emotional mind is robbing you of is to just sit still for a few minutes and *pretend that we have died.* In that state, we do not need thoughts of the past or worries of the future. We can just exist. In that moment, one will feel complete peace and joy as one transcends one's mind and enters into *awareness* devoid of any internal dialogue or thoughts. That is where we perceive the "flower behind the mirror (of mind)" that enlightened souls have referred to.

This is so because the mind stops reflecting what the world presents to us and we find our true identity, the core inner higher self. By existing in this, we start perceiving oneness with everything around us as if the energy within and outside have united as the outer layers have been shed. It appears as if one has expanded in time and space and become one with the energy of the Universe. It is definitely the most wonderful experience one can have.

~

When I first experienced complete bliss and feeling of universal union, I was compelled to research similar experiences by others and ancient texts regarding this truth. One such understanding came to me from the *Advaita* (without duality) *Vedanta*, a Hindu school of philosophy which combines three ancient revered texts: the *Upanishads, Bhagavad Gita* and *Brahma Sutra*; collectively referred to as *Prasthanatrayi*. It strives to help humans exist in a state referred to as *"Sat-chit-anand,"* a state of complete divine bliss connected with our higher selves and its divine connections.

According to its study, the human body exists as three types of bodies (*Sharira* in Sanskrit) and in five layers (*Koshas* in Sanskrit) and with realisation gets expanded to seven layers (*Koshas* or Sheaths or Mantle: like curtains) as it accesses the sublime, divine, infinite and eternal Universal Power.

Three types of bodies Shariras:

1. Gross *(Sthula Sharira)*,
2. Astral *(Linga Sharira)*,
3. Causal Body *(Karana Sharira)*.

Five types of layers Panch Kosha:

1. *Annamaya* (food)
2. *Pranamaya* (air energy)
3. *Manomaya* (mind)
4. *Vigyanmaya* (intellect) and
5. *Anandamaya (bliss)*.

The seeker is taught to perceive and transcend each layer to reach the core of one's existence. Once we perceive the *Anandamaya Kosha*, we experience peace at our very core (located in the heart region). We can take this experience further and enter the next two layers of existence*: Chitta and Sat Koshas*. If we are able to exist in complete stillness and consciousness, an awareness arises of an energised joyous force (*Chitta Kosha*) in the core or centre of our being. This is the realisation of the true self, the soul (*Atman*). By simply staying in that state and uniting with the surroundings as we have shed by transcendence all our outer layers, the soul connects with the powers of the Supreme Universal Power and its Energy (*Sat Kosha*).

The feeling of infinity and eternity dawns on us which are the most uplifting, rejuvenating, divine and glorious feeling of ecstasy worthy of experiencing by one and all. This connection with universal energy comes with infinite and eternal love, wisdom and strength which helps us in creating our own destiny. Hence, in that state the human entity and the Powers of Universe combine to create the future, also referred to as *Yatinam Brahma Bhavati Sarathi*. This is only possible for those who have the qualities of complete honesty and pure intent to ensure only good intentions are carried out by use of these powers. It is easy to realise how wonderfully peaceful and harmonious such a society will be, undoubtedly beneficial to the entire mankind. In essence, this state of existence, i.e., *Sat-chit-anand,* denotes:

Existing in super consciousness blissfully in union with our pure higher self, in sync with the infinite eternal Supreme energy and its creation.

A State of Pure Intent, Conciousness, and Complete Harmony.

In that state the subject and object of our perception become one and unites the creative energy of our life force with that of the Universe.

Although the explanation offered in this philosophy/science seems supernatural, it indeed is absolutely true when one experiences it. A simpler way to look and appreciate this realisation might be to take a moment to understand this carefully and experience each aspect of your complete being:

1. Look at yourself in the mirror from head to toe, and our *outer body* is obvious. The layer of energy along the physical body is the *Annamaya Kosha.*
2. Take a deep breath, and feel the air circulate in your systems. Feel your *inner body*. The energy bathing the organ systems with air and circulation is the *Pranamaya Kosha.*
3. Examine the thoughts that are arising in your brain, referred to as the *mind*. And the background noise in your head which keeps having thoughts and emotions about "me" or "my" relationships or "my" circumstance or "my" life situation...and gives you feelings of fear or sadness or anger or disgust...that is the ego part of the *mind*. The sum total of all these is referred to as the *Manomaya Kosha.*
4. Do the math: two plus two; that is the *intelligence* within you. It comprehends and applies logic to find solutions. This is referred to as the *Vigyanmaya Kosha.*
5. And when you put all of your mind's processes to a standstill. You suddenly emerge as a peaceful entity, which is the close reflection of your *soul* where it borders with your *mind*. It is the *super-conscious*, which always exists in peace and bliss. This is referred to as the *Anandamaya Kosha.*
6. Feel the stillness at the core of your existence, in the heart area, without any thoughts while in the state of peaceful state described in para-5 above; that is your consciousness, awareness of your soul. This is referred to as the *Chitta Kosha.*
7. Stay in the above state patiently, and with complete belief and faith and love in the Supreme Universal Power, harmonise with its creation; that is the *divine, supreme, infinite Eternal Bliss*. This is referred to as the *Sat Kosha.*

This union with the Supreme Power is denied to all who do not have a Pure Intent, and are motivated by selfish desires without feelings of compassion and service.

The access is restricted until feelings of selfless service consume an individual so as to prevent any misuse of power.

But once you have seen yourself in totality, you can appreciate that your ego-driven mind had taken over your life with continuously distracting thoughts. Such thoughts can arise at the rate of 20-40 per minute! Having reached this realisation of our totality, and having brought our racing mind to a standstill, we can enjoy complete peace within. And with practice perceive our infinite and eternal connections which allow us to live in complete bliss.

That is the state of *Salvation* we achieve when we have rid ourselves of the tormenting thoughts in our mind and achieved unity with the all powerful, comforting, peaceful and joyful energy and power of the Universe. Interestingly, this state is also the desired state of existence preached by other sections in the world, referred to as *Moksha* in Hinduism, *Nirvana* in Buddhism. With the simple realisation of existing in a state of quiet mind in super-consciousness, we can connect to the powers of the universe. With that power, we can access and do anything...as long as it vibrates with the laws of the universe, the most important of which is compassion...

Super-consciousness: a state of awareness of ourselves with a quiet alert consciousness; where the ego-driven emotional mind is inactive, the intelligence is alert, and observational consciousness is sharp.

And the only thing we have to do is to *Quieten Our Ego-driven, Emotional Minds and stop having thoughts about me and I...*

The reason it becomes easy to stop thinking through our ego-driven mind is because we recognise that it is a very small part of mind and it restricts us sometimes to the point of stifling us. By accessing the universal mind, we have access to so much higher energy and potential that it takes care of all our problems without causing us distress. The problems are solved easily because we gain infinite wisdom and courage to address any and every issue that we confront. Our vibrations are immediately elevated from suffering to liberation!

Another practice wherein an individual is constantly situated in a state of peace is referred to as *"Soto Zazen."* This is a practice that some Buddhists in Japan practice to the extent that it becomes a lifestyle. It was initially brought into Japan by Dogen Zenji from China. The Zen practice is an offshoot of Mahayana Buddhism from northern parts of East Asia. Buddha taught about the five *Shandhas* (aggregates or aspects of humans: *Rupa, Vedana, Samjna, Samskara, Vijnana*), of which the highest was consciousness (*Vijnana).* However, the original practice stems from the *Dhyana Yoga* (Focus and Meditation) described in Chapter 6 of the *Bhagavad Gita*, a Hindu scripture. This was altered to Ch'an in China and Zen in Japan as pronunciation changed with accent.

Irrespective of the name used, the practice is to simply sit in a straight posture looking straight ahead and merely noticing whatever lies ahead. It is almost like an open eye meditation. The difference is that you can do it all day! To practise Zen, one sits or does whatever we need to without thinking about anything. The amazing part is that it is not difficult to get to an enlightened state many times in a day! In that peaceful state, one can sit undisturbed for a long time, enjoying the pure joy of being.

This state is also what is referred to by the term, "*Sat Chit Anand"* or *Shiv Yog* (Shiv: *Lord Shiva*, who is part of the Hindu *Trinity* and is considered to be an all-powerful, auspicious one who transforms and destroys evil; *Yog:* Union). In such a state, saints are able to perceive their higher, true, peaceful, wise, and loving identities in a deep trance-like meditative state. Essentially, it is switching off the mental thinking and then feeling; allowing them to perceive and hear through their energised souls.

It is a realisation that sinks deep into our core,
not in the brain, but in the heart.

Each second appears to be a snap shot of infinity, and each
cell of ours participates in the energy of the moment.

When our entire being synchronises with all there is, "we" melt and become one with the Universe. The manifest unites with the unmanifest, seen with the unseen, form with formless...and in that state, Man meets the powers of the Universe.

When we lose the sense of duality of us and others, our thoughts, words and actions stop bearing any reactive component. All decisions, words, actions that come out of this space is "*non-karmic*" or does not have the usual worldly action-reaction effect because they are prompted by the emotion of the Supreme...and this is the path to a life of complete *bliss*!

Why would we deny ourselves such a beautiful feeling? Why does the emotional mind rob us of this state? The answer is: *because the ego-mind feels threatened by individuals or circumstances and feels a need to remain in constant action for the sake of perceived survival.* The only thing that is threatened by this state of bliss is the ego-driven emotional mind, which is not essential for human survival anyways! It is the part of mind created by our society and that only promotes egoistic survival.

But in That Process of Creating a Seperate Identity from Our Soul,

Our Ego Robs Us of All Our Innate Ability to Create, Learn, Love, Enjoy, and Live in Peace.

And once we let go of attachment to thoughts arising from this mind, our innate survival instincts to protect us from physical threats remain intact, in fact, even more ready due to our focus in the present. It is sheer madness to let a very small aspect of our existence, our emotional minds, and take over our perfect state of existence. A state of existence that has the capability to connect with the powers of the Universe. Why would we choose to isolate ourselves into "I," which is like a single drop from the ocean verses eliminating the "I" and becoming one with the Ocean? If this state of existence is so peaceful and joyous, what can we do to be in that state constantly? Iyenger, a highly acclaimed *Yogi,* who resides in Pune, India, has said it very well:

Enlightenment is being thoughtfully thoughtless."

— Iyenger

And once again, the simplest and most effective way to experience that peaceful nature of true self is to pretend the 'you' (as perceived by your ego) is dead! In that state you can obviously not have any thoughts about 'yourself'. In so doing, you completely shut off your ego-driven emotional mind, the rest of you becomes alive, and your true life force shines through!

In essence, we have to stop living in a world of thoughts and start living in the world of reality. Right here, right now! It is morbidity and craziness to live any other way! It is funny that this truth has been screaming at us for centuries.

~

Additional Universal Wisdom for Chapter 4

Old Testament Bible

Isaiah 26:3

"You will keep in perfect peace him whose mind is steadfast, because he trusts in you."

Bhagavad Gita:

Chapter 3, Verse 42-43.

"The working senses are superior to dull matter; mind is higher than the senses; intelligence is still higher than the mind; and he [the soul] is even higher than the intelligence.

Thus, knowing oneself to be transcendental to material senses, mind and intelligence, one should control the lower self by the higher self and thus—by spiritual strength—conquer this insatiable enemy known as lust."

Chapter 6:20-23

"The stage of perfection is called samadhi, when one's mind is completely restrained from material mental activities by practice of yoga. This is characterised by one's ability to see the self by the pure mind and to relish and rejoice in the self.

In that joyous state, one is situated in boundless transcendental happiness and enjoys himself through transcendental senses. Established thus, one never departs from the truth and upon gaining this he thinks there is no greater gain.

Being situated in such a position, one is never shaken, even in the midst of greatest difficulty. This indeed is actual freedom from all miseries arising from material contact."

New Testament Bible:

James 3:17-18

"Who is wise and understanding among you? Let him show it by his good life, by deeds done in the humility that comes from wisdom. But if you harbour bitter envy and selfish ambition in your hearts, do not boast about it or deny the truth. Such "wisdom" does not come down from heaven but is earthly, unspiritual, of the devil. For where you have envy and selfish ambition, there you find disorder and every evil practice. But the wisdom that comes from heaven is first of all pure; then peace loving, considerate, submissive, full of mercy and good fruit, impartial and sincere. Peacemakers, who sow in peace, raise a harvest of righteousness."

Romans 12:2

"Do not be conformed to this world, but be transformed by the renewal of your mind, that by testing you may discern what is the will of God, what is good and acceptable and perfect."

2 Timothy 1:7

"For God gave us a spirit not of fear but of power and love and self-control."

Dhammapada: 205

"Having tasted the sweetness of inner solitude and calmness, he who lives by the Law is free from fear and suffering."

Dhammapada:

Chapter 3

"It is good to tame the mind which is difficult to hold in and flighty, rushing wherever it listeth; a tamed mind brings happiness."

Qur'an:

Surat Qâf [50:22]

(And it will be said). "You were certainly in unmindfulness of this, and we have removed from you your cover, so your sight, this Day, is sharp."

Al-Maidah [5:16]

"By which Allah guides those, who pursue His pleasure to the ways of peace and brings them out from darknesses into the light, by His permission, and guides them to a straight path."

Sri Guru Granth Sahib:

Page 6

"See the brotherhood of all mankind as the highest order of Yogis; conquer your own mind, and conquer the world."

Page 87

"As the self realises, enlightenment grows without effort".

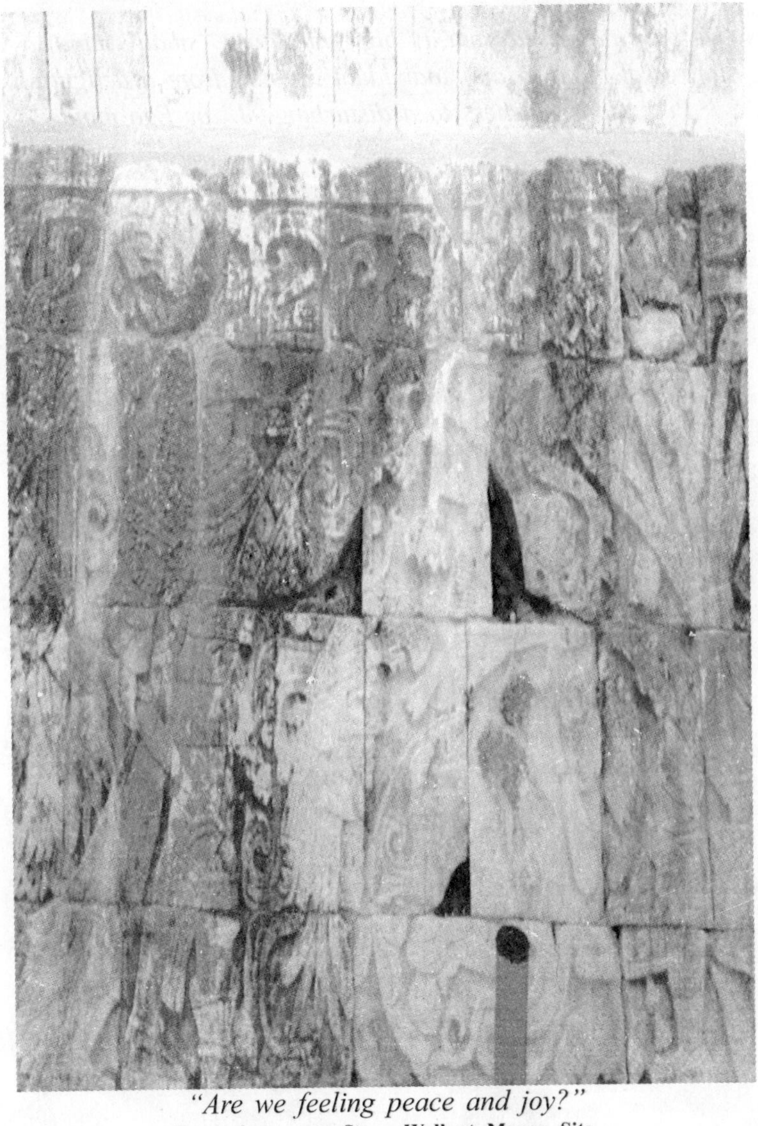

"Are we feeling peace and joy?"
Engravings on a Stone Wall at Mayan Site.

If we are not feeling bliss, then we have lost insight of our true identity, which is to be in sync with the universe.

We have regressed from a "big" mind to a "small" mind; a universal mind to an "individual" mind....from a delightful Pure Consciousness to a disturbing "I" or Ego mind.

5

To Be or Not to Be

It is an wonderful realisation that in spite of being aware of the insanity associated with living each moment lost in thoughts about "I" or "me," humans continue to do so. It appears that man's greatest fear in letting go of his or her "I" is often associated with the fear of losing "identity". People argue, "What will I be if I don't think of myself!"

But the question arises, who are we? Are we our body, mind or soul? We know that our body will decay and perish, resulting in eventual physical demise. We know that our mind is restless and will not let us live in peace. Then why should we perceive self as soul? If I am my soul, then I know that it is an immortal energy of my life force and is connected to the energy of the universe. Then why do I need to constantly think, or worry, or be fearful about its safety, worthiness, acceptance, or mortality?

With this realisation comes the awareness that "I" do not have to be something special to be fulfilled. In fact, the best way to exist is to just acknowledge whatever you are in this moment. The sum total of the past moments has brought you to this moment, and we just have to ungrudgingly accept it. By accepting this moment and ourselves, we become so peaceful and joyous that it actually becomes empowering to undertake the right thoughts needed for the present, which will result in the right words and actions. These right actions in the present will become the road to the future. And as someone has rightly said:

"Today is the tomorrow of yesterday that you worried about and the yesterday of tomorrow that you feared!"

Every moment offers us an opportunity to live in an enlightened state of alert and awake, yet quiet and peaceful, consciousness.

If we do not do it, it is because of our own wrong choice of living in a pseudo-world of thoughts rather than the truth of the present moment.

Therein our natural peaceful and joyful state changes into distress and strife.

It cannot be said better than these words of a wise person:

"We sow our thoughts, and we reap our actions.

We sow our actions, and we reap our habits.

We sow our habits and we reap our characters.

We sow our characters, and we reap our destiny."

It is in the state of true "being" (focussed in the moment) rather than "not being" (lost in thoughts) that one is most creative, energised, and productive. Without being personal, one is most personable! The reason is simple...

In that state of existence, we access the core of existence, the energy of life force that is beyond the mind.

And through it one becomes truly connected to the energies of the entire universe.

The energies of the universe bring with it a feeling of love that fills us with peace and joy.

It also connects us to the higher wisdom and courage to do .vhat is needed in the moment.

When we recognise our true higher selves and start existing under the guidance of our core energy source, we feel and understand how we are the smaller manifestation of a bigger manifestation, the Universe. We also comprehend that we have the acceptance of the universe because we are an integral part of it. As an integral part of it, we blend into it, so there is no awkwardness in what we are and what we have to offer. And if we desire to create and change our circumstance for a more satisfying experience, *we have the resources of the universe to our benefit, if we abide by the laws of the universe.*

In its simplest form, this law is the rule of compassion, the Golden Rule: treat others as you want to be treated.

Obedience to this law of compassion or the golden rule is of paramount importance, because if energy is used against the laws of synchrony and sustenance of the universe by a unit of its (Universe) own energy, that will cause disharmony and disturbance. This will generate a negative or deficit in the energy field of that unit (also referred to "*Karmic*" field for a human action in Hinduism).

Hence, action (Karma) guided by righteousness (following the Golden Rule of compassion, also referred to as Dharma) is the simplistic and most fulfilling way of living life.

However, our ego-driven mind often takes over our thoughts, words and actions by self-imposing its non-sensical, and selfish thinking. The result is that we are led astray with greed, lust, jealousy, hate, anger, pride, and deceit, which provide an anti-thesis to the Golden Rule.

.~.

In essence, if a soul (which by its inherent original nature is truth, peace, love, joy, wisdom, courage and purity) is influenced to undertake negative actions by a disarrayed mind (conditioned, circumstantial, influenced by ego perceptions) for the pleasures of body and mind, one gets associated with actions against the laws of synchrony of the Universe. *The result is that one earns karmic debt,* the consequences of which can be horrendous and long-lasting. *The law of the Universe if broken will bring with it negative consequences, just as the law of the land does.*

In living a life guided by principles that are contradictory to the harmonious and synchronised laws of the universe, we earn negative energy or karmic debts.

The compulsion to break the law of compassion comes out of the greed, lust, hate, jealousy, and revenge brewing in the ego-driven mind.

These karmic debts will manifest as mental or physical distress and diseases, hurtful circumstances, etc., culminating in suffering.

Therefore, the most important role of any human is to identify its own true identity, the soul, and keep it clear of attacks from its own ego-driven mind.

JUST BY DOING SO, we will be able to live peacefully and enjoy, create, and express our purpose and reap the soul's fulfillment on Earth.

This fulfillment comes from living righteously, learning, laughing and loving!

Therein comes the realisation that life is a divine experience and simply a journey of the soul in this world.

The body and mind are mere layers of convenience around our true self, the soul.

This may sound simple, but to experience it sometimes becomes a challenge, especially by overtly analytical thinking, or egoistic minds. That is so, since the soul is hidden and unmanifest while the mind is always keeping us wrapped in thoughts. Hence, one has to transcend our thought-laden mind to access the soul, which becomes obscure and dormant in an entity, wherein the mind becomes hyper-active. This is similar to a situation in which a wonderful picture stays hidden by constant smoke (stream of thoughts) arising out of a burning log (overactive mind). And yet, considering that the soul is indeed our pure and true identity, we have to find ways to encounter that life force within ourselves.

What good would our lives be if we do not meet ourselves! So, we are not what we think we are, and we should not be what we are not. And yet we need to be what we truly are, but first we have to know ourselves! And the amazing discovery stemming from a simple realisation shows us that we carry in our higher self the blueprint and life's plan for us. Not unlike the DNA in the nucleus of our cells. In that inner core, we have the wisdom, courage, and energy to lead the best life possible, full of good health and satisfying success. The key to exist in peace and the capability to live and enjoy everything with truth and love becomes apparent.

Once the realisation dawns on us of our true nature, a still, peaceful, and joyous being in the core of our existence, we can be just that and not what we have been used to in the past; an unsteady, tormented, distressed, and despair-prone individual. The choice becomes very easy: to simply be what we truly and originally are and not what we become in this world! It is astonishing that this truth has been beckoning us for thousands of years and that we have continued to be aloof to it!

.~.

Additional Universal Wisdom for Chapter 5

Old Testament Bible:

1 Samuel 16:7

"But the Lord said to Samuel, "Do not look on his appearance or on the height of his stature, because I have rejected him. For the Lord sees not as man sees: man looks on the outward appearance, but the Lord looks on the heart."

Bhagavad Gita:

Chapter 3, Verse 34.

"Attraction and repulsion for sense objects are felt by embodied beings, but one should not fall under the control of senses and sense objects because they are stumbling blocks on the path of self-realisation."

Chapter 3, Verse 39-40

"Thus, a man's pure consciousness is covered by his eternal enemy in the form of lust, which is never satisfied and which burns like fire."

"The senses, the mind and the intelligence are the sitting places of this lust, which veils the real knowledge of the living entity and bewilders him".

New Testament Bible:

Peter 3:3-4

"Do not let your adorning be external—the braiding of hair and the putting on of gold jewellery, or the clothing you wear— but

let your adorning be the hidden person of the heart with the imperishable beauty of a gentle and quiet spirit, which in God's sight is very precious."

Dhammapada: 239

"As a silversmith removes dust from silver, so the wise man rids himself gradually of all his impurities."

Qur'an:

Ash-Shams 91:9

"He has succeeded who purifies it (the soul)."

Sri Guru Granth Sahib:

Page 415

"The foolish mind is perverted and greedy.....

Understanding itself, this soul becomes attuned to the Formless Lord.

This mind becomes immaculately pure, in the Court and the Home of the Lord."

.~.

Commanding and Forbidding Wall and Steps.

The greatest tragedy for any man is to not realise his true self. Unfortunately, this tragedy will not end with his physical death.

However, as soon as we break the chains of slavery to our "I" mind and release all fear, anxiety, hate, jealousy, resentment that we were subjected to by our "Ego-mind," we become liberated and taste the sweetness of human soul's freedom.

Therein the only emotion that remains is the one that truly matters: love.

6

The Ultimate Freedom and Liberty

For most individuals in this world today, our lives have become so complicated and *disheveled* that we are unable to truly be peaceful and enjoy life as we were intended to. There is a feeling of bondage, heaviness, unrest, anxiety, or distress that haunts us in the background of our minds. Pleasures of the body and mind only distract us temporarily. We are just not able to feel *free* once we have entered the life cycle of physical manifestation on earth.

For this state of uneaseness, we blame our condition, using stories about personal achievements, family, social or work issues. Or it relates to concerns of our relationships with relatives, children, parents, friends, or colleagues. The list is never ending...with so much to be concerned about, how can we feel free?

The simple solution lies in recognising that:

1. Every feeling has a thought behind it;
2. Thoughts are created by the mind;
3. If we live in the thoughts-driven mind, we are not living in the present moment;
4. Since only the present is true, by living lost in thoughts, we are living in a pseudo or false world;
5. If we live in a false world immersed in thoughts, we cannot truly live life or solve any problems in the present;

6. On the other hand, if we live in the present only, then we can live life fully and take care of whatever needs attention;
7. When the time arrives to attend to a concern in the future, we will be guided by our inner wisdom to address it at that moment;
8. We have to be free of thoughts of the past and future, which, as it is, do not exist in the present;
9. In such a state we are peaceful, full of energy, creative, and connected with our highest-self;
10. Alert in that awareness, we perceive all the energy around us and access the wisdom of the universe from within by the soul's infinite and eternal connections!

Therefore, to become truly "free" and liberated one needs to simply empty one's mind. A simple realisation that the world of thoughts is actually an untrue world, created by our own mind and reflecting its own attitude, suddenly opens up a new awareness of self. This awareness starts growing in our daily lives and with time and experience can become our lifestyle. What is amazing is that it comes with a feeling of immense lightness and clarity that almost feels like a new life. A transformed life to lead our best life possible!

Guru Nanak Devji beautifully said,

"Realisation of Truth is higher than all else. Higher still is truthful living." In seeking the higher-self, logic will not work—only understanding will. The most important aspect is NOT to try and describe it in words, because the feeling is beyond any language. One has to experience it. Even these words such as "feeling" and "experience" cannot do justice to that states...it is indefinable.

A beautiful feeling of lightness ensues and one feels completely refreshed as if born again!

~

It is liberation of self from the chains of slavery to the ego-mind. The feeling of freedom is like a release from a stifling place, as if we were holding our breath under water and have come up for air after a very long time! It is not unlike the feeling of losing a bag of foul smelling garbage that we carry on our back (metaphor for thoughts in ego-mind) all the time, full of sorry morbid tales of fear, anxiety, past and future. And on discarding that garbage baggage, peace and joy ensues as we enter the fresh, wonderful realisation of the present.

One feels as if one has gone from a very suffocating and squished space to an open, large, and limitless place. And yet it is not a defined space, it is *ALL and EVERYTHING!* This feeling is not unlike a ray of light realising its connections with the sun! Like a drop of ocean, joined the ocean and expanded in form tc that of the ocean! Once you experience it, it is unmistakably the most wonderful way to exist. And you are every bit entitled to it, and guaranteed to get it…you just have to sit still and stop thinking! You will be able to see everything around you crystal clear as if looking at a vibrant picture, where everything is important and yet nothing matters anymore!

The importance of liberation of the soul from the torments of the ego-driven mind has been recognised from times immemorial. The Spiritual richness of the East, with its accompanying promise of peace, in comparison to the materialistic compassion of the West, associated with mental distress, has been long known to humanity. In the quest for spiritual realisation it is not uncommon for many men and women to undertake celibacy and retreat from family life early and meditate on the word of God. That extremely desirous state of peace and bliss was recognised in many terminologies in the East, and varied in its spectrum of experience, which led a soul to be in a liberated state: *Moksha, Nirvana*, Enlightenment etc.

A practice highly recommended for that purpose was: *meditate with pure intent and consciousness to reach awareness beyond the mind* also referred to as *Sadhana*. Various methods were suggested to rise above the ever-busy mind not uncommonly found to be full of thoughts. One such option suggested was *Mantra* recitation at defined times or while undertaking any task or at any time where mind feels disturbed. *"Mantra"* means "Mind liberation" and it denotes a practice of using word or words, or hymns, or prayers that symbolise unity with the higher power. It was suggested that such a *Mantra* be recited loudly initially but eventually silently in the mind. Surely this is a good way to keep the mind away from the path of getting distracted and taking off to another time (past of future), or situations that are not meaningful at present. Essentially this simple method of keeping thoughts in check is not unlike using a computer screen saver to conserve energy and having a safety software downloaded on the computer to protect from harmful threats. The most wonderful aspect of such practices is that not only do we conserve mental energy for intellectual purposes, prevent distracting thoughts resulting in sharper focus, but are also able to have a deep observation power and keep in touch with our higher self.

An even more extensive and perpetual practice to keep mind pure is to focus on breathing to divert the mind from going into its pseudo-world of ego-driven thoughts of past and future. Considering Man breathes 15-20 times a minute, and similar is the frequency of thoughts (or higher in some active minds), one can divert the mind on to breathing rather than give it time and opportunity to think negatively. In this way, the mind can stay where the body is, rather than scattering all over in time and space and bringing with that scatter a plethora of unwanted feelings.

Alternatively, one can merely be completely engrossed in the current landscape or whatever is in front and around us at any given moment.

Ultimately, it is with this practice that one exists constantly in a blissful state of being continuously and consciously engaged in the present moment with a pure and fresh mind!

One reaches a magical and mystical state of existence of complete transcendence. That is the state of what I like to refer as *"awareness of quiet alert consciousness"*. In that state, we continuously stay in a peaceful and undisturbed existence, allowing our higher self to be free of any torments of our lower self !

It was in that state of awareness that I perceived two words of immense significance, as if the dancing winds whispered the wisdom of the grounds of Chichen Itza, the Mayan ruins, on December 22nd, 2012 afternoon.

.~.

Additional Universal Wisdom for Chapter 6

Old Testament Bible:

Isaiah 26:3

"You will keep in perfect peace him whose mind is steadfast, because he trusts in you."

Psalm 34:14

"Turn from evil and do good. Seek peace and pursue it."

Bhagavad Gita:

Chapter 5, Verse 27-28

"Shutting out all external sense objects, keeping the eyes and vision concentrated between the two eyebrows, suspending the inward and outward breaths within the nostrils—thus controlling the mind, senses and intelligence, the transcendentalist becomes free from desire, fear and anger. One who is always in this state is certainly liberated."

Chapter 2, Verse 15

"The person who is not disturbed by happiness and distress and is steady in both is certainly eligible for liberation."

New Testament Bible:

John 8:32

"Then you will know the truth and the truth will set you free."

John 14:27

"Peace I leave with you; my peace I give you. I do not give to you as the world gives. Do not let your hearts be troubled and do not be afraid."

Sutta Nipata:

948

"Desire is a chain, shackled to the world, and it is a difficult one to break. But once that is done, there is no more grief and no more longing; the stream has been cut off and there are no more chains."

Qur'an:

Al-Baqarah 2:256

"Truth has been made clear from error. Whoever rejects false worship and believes in God has grasped the trustworthiness hand-hold that never breaks. And God hears and knows all things."

Sri Guru Granth Sahib:

Page 11

"They are liberated, they are liberated—those who meditate on the Lord. For them, the noose of death is cut away.

Those who meditate on the Fearless One, on the Fearless Lord—all their fears are dispelled."

.~.

More Mayan Carvings and Structures Telling Stories.

Just one taste of our true peaceful state compels us to seek it again and again because living any other way is stifling.

In this new liberated and free state we start identifying and synchronising with the entire universe. Guided by the principles of the universe, our creativity, wisdom, and joy know no bounds.

Situated in such a state, each being has access to powers of the universe to bring joy and glory to the universe and its creative energy.

7

Two Words of Wisdom

I looked around from the back seat of the coach that was taking us from Cancun to Chichen Itza, in order to see the Mayan ruins, on that fateful day. Suddenly, the afternoon light seemed to get brighter and it felt as if I was looking through a telescope. And then abruptly a feeling came that I could see myself at the other end of the telescope!

On that sunny and peaceful day, the air was crisp and grounds alive with the buzz of human energy. The serenity of the sacred site was well-preserved by the empirical monuments, despite the humble and unassuming land. The majestic pyramidal shaped temple, with its steep steps and symbolic snake and lion figurate, was an amazing sight to behold. The expansive playground and sculptured walls seemed to be still whispering historical values. The teeming crowd, curiously inspecting and searching for answers, was positioned around knowledgeable guides. It appeared that they all were synchronously tuning into ancient wisdom. This picture of life, blending past and present, suddenly unfolded an amazing epiphany and the revelation froze my entire being. It seemed as if the wind had picked up the wisdom from the earth, and was whispering it into my heart. I had just woken up after a brief nap on the bus ride and my mind was blank as if fresh and ready to receive… and the compelling message revealed by the scene on the holy grounds was obvious. Just two words of wisdom that reverberated with my years of research for the truth. The two words I perceived in that mystical state were clear, crisp yet soft, firm and authoritative. And they rang in my ears, mind and heart simultaneously for some time: *"Be One"*. I jolted, with the words playing repeatedly in my being, not sure if I was trying to comprehend the experience correctly.

Internally, it felt just right to sit with it without trying to explain it. And the feeling was of such immense peace and joy amounting to bliss, that I did not want to even stir lest I misplace the feeling. But as I moved on with life and others around me, I felt as if I was in a trance and disconnected from, and yet completely connected with everything. And the reason it was so compelling was that it was the most perfect moment to be in!

Sometimes words cannot explain nor do justice to a phenomenon. In fact, words may deter a realisation because they lead us to comprehension of a concept in our head, although what may be required is a feeling in our core, in the heart, circulating in our entire being. The state of true happiness is an experience when the body, mind, and soul completely connect in an existence of quiet consciousness and awareness. And through that awareness we are connected to everything around us.

My own experience with the feeling induced by the message was very different from the spiritual experiences I had undergone in the past. I suddenly felt completely one with everything and everyone around me... and it felt as if the ground and the sky had united their ancient wisdom and unfolded it as: *Be One.* The experience of complete synchrony with that blissful reflection was laced with a sense of rejoicing and elation. There was an upsurge of feeling of love for everything around me, which completely washed away any resentment, hurt, concerns, fear, dismay... and brought about a peaceful smile on my face. And with each heart beat I felt deep and sincere gratitude towards the power that had endowed me with this realisation.

At the surface and limited to the 'finite mind', these two words cannot produce all those feelings. Nor can they have any lasting effect to transform a moment, let alone a life! That would be counter-productive to what is intended by this book. To perceive, realise, and endorse this feeling to the extent that one starts living with it, one has to access the 'infinite mind.' The "small" mind has to give in to the "big" mind. And it all starts with a simple process of creating a blank mind.

Once in that state, carefully read the paragraph below and *feel* each word. Not much needs to be said anyways, but elaborations will be made to ensure the point drives home...into the heart...and it will start a realisation that will grow with time and bring us to exist in our true identities. In that state, we will discover the essence of life and our purpose on earth.

To be one is to be united. We all know that in unity there is strength. But amazingly in unity of our body, mind, and soul there is a feeling of complete acceptance of everything, and resultant peace and bliss, indescribable and priceless, along with a deep sense of knowing, freedom, compassion, and gratitude.

The body feels rested, the mind is quiet and present with the body in the current time and space, and a peaceful, joyful soul beamingly smiles equipped with the wisdom of the universe, free and ready to undertake any challenge!

And if there are no challenges in the present moment, then one would just "be" and "enjoy being".

.~.

This is a state that you would not want to miss being in, it is worth "dying" for! And the only "dying" that has to occur is at the level of the ego!

For us to experience that *pure complete bliss*, we have to be *pure in intent and consciousness*, unadulterated by any thoughts and *completely present in body, mind and soul in that moment in terms of time and space*. One cannot experience pure bliss if one is not pure in intent, that is, with no ulterior or scheming motives. And one cannot experience complete bliss until one is completely present in the moment to feel it. There has to be unity within and all around.

(I) Be one with yourself:

Body-Mind-Soul Unity is *prima facie* true, valid, or sufficient at first impression, wherein one keeps all their attention and awareness in the same time and space as the body. All the mental faculties: observation, consciousness, intelligence, thoughts need to be in the same experiential zone as the body at any given moment. Life then becomes a continuously changing landscape and:

Each moment offers an opportunity to live in a liberated state of awareness and to achieve an existence of enlightenment.

With repeated practice, we start existing continuously in a deeper realisation of our true higher selves in complete pure bliss.

Among the various practices that can help us achieve this very simply is the "Zen" practice. This was originally taken from the teachings of Buddha from Hindu scriptures of "*Dhyana Yoga*" or union through meditation and focus. Thereafter, it has been refined into its current practice. In very simple terms, one may look at it as follows:

(i) **Adopt the right posture:** Irrespective of where you are, always try to look ahead or at whatever present in front of you with an upright posture. In this manner, the mind stays where the body is and does not deflect to any other thoughts, except focussing in the now.

(ii) **Have the right attitude:** Knowing that we are the soul and immortal, irrespective of what happens to our body or mental achievements, we start continue living in peace. By understanding that even the mind has more than one aspect: intelligence, observational, "ego-emotions", and subconscious and super-conscious awareness, one is liberated from mental lock-up. This prevents us from staying stuck in the "ego-driven emotional mind". Therein we recognise that associating with thoughts of "me" and "I" is complete insanity. We move away from insanity into sanity, from distress to peace as we start existing with the right attitude of soul consciousness.

(iii) **Apply the right understanding:** Realising that only the present moment is true, the rest are all *mind created* thoughts, we can comfortably be present in the now and stay with the truth. In that truthful existence, we can fully experience and address our life with our body, mind and soul. The right understanding teaches us the essence of complete focus in the moment.

(iv) **Knowledge and practice:** Understanding the truth about ourselves, which is to know our soul, we recognise our birth-right to live as blissful entities with wisdom and courage. In this soul-conscious state, we now just have to apply the inner-wisdom to draft the principles of life.

(a) *One in Time, Body-Mind-Soul:* Stay in the present moment, because all experiences and fulfillment will be in this present moment. This moment is everything; the future of the previous moment and past of the next moment. As a wise man once said, "The secret of health for both mind and body is not to mourn for the past, worry about the future, or anticipate troubles but to live in the present moment wisely and earnestly."

(b) *One in Space, Body-Mind-Soul:* Completely synchronise with the surroundings, seeing yourself as a part of that environment. Only in this equilibrium and harmony will the energies unite to bring and synchronously help manifest the positive experiences.

(II) Be One with The One:

If an energy is left by itself, it will have no power to grow and eventually will be drained. Hence, once we discover that our true identity is our *higher self* or *soul*, we have to connect it to the energy and power source of origin. By being mindful of the fact that the Universe has been created and is sustained by a Power that is referred to in this book at various points as: Universal Power, Supreme Power, or God, one can connect with that source of its Energy and become ever-renewing and infinitely powerful. Since, this Power has created and now sustains the universe, it has limitless potential. Through our connection with it, we can leave all our concerns of future on it. All we need to focus then on is doing our best in the present moment. And that is only possible by harmoniously working with the surroundings, seeing yourself as a part of that environment, and working in union for mutual benefit.

This *unity within and outside* is probably the *sine qua non* for any orderly and meaningful human existence. The phrase *sine qua non* according to the dictionary stands for *something absolutely indispensable or essential.* Otherwise, we will continue to live in a disordered, discordant, disruptive and distressful state both with self and others and miss out on the most beautiful experience of our lives. Therefore, we *owe* this practice to others and ourselves and should start living with the implementation of the realisation to "*Be One*" with self and surroundings, treating each other with love and respect reflecting invincible compassion.

·~·

"Do unto others as you would have them do unto you."

— Jesus of Nazareth

"If you want others to be happy practice compassion. If you want to be happy practice compassion."

—Dalai Lama

"Only a life lived for others is a life worthwhile"

—Albert Einstein

Provision for others is a fundamental responsibility of human life."

— Woodrow Wilson

Can you imagine living with that feeling all the time, with everyone reciprocating that feeling....would that not be Paradise on Earth! And with it comes the amazing power to co-create our destiny following righteousness in equilibrium with the Universe. This is a phenomenon referred to as *Brahma Bhavati Sarathi*.

Just as a selfish, unrighteous and cannibalistic nature can spread like disease destroying the peace and tranquility of the world and eventually making it extinct, similarly the right intervention, like a vaccine, or naturally immune individuals, can stop the toxic spread of devastation caused by dysfunctional human mind. Unfortunately in such a state, each of those imbalanced minds will have to undergo much suffering equivalent to, or maybe even more than, what they have themselves caused. Eventually, the whole human race will be burning with anguish and despair with no relief in sight.

.~.

It is indeed unfortunate that the very philosophy, i.e., religion, which was intended to help us experience the union within self, with others, and with the Supreme power, has created a divide among humans. On the other hand, a deeper look into the different religions should help us realise, how this is a baseless hassle created again by our egoistic mind. If we look carefully we should recognise that all major religions have in some ways originated from future generations of a common pool of humans, who have migrated over period of time to different places. Along the way revelations have come to humans in different places at different times in different human forms. The core teaching of all religions is essentially the same: peace, joy, and love for humanity. Then how can it be claimed that any particular religion has intention of war, distress, and hate for another person or religion. Is it not hypocritical to say that we are spiritual or religious and be intolerant of another faith or person? Is this misunderstanding from inadequate knowledge and wisdom? Or are these imposed on our society by individuals or organisations that benefit themselves by keeping us divided for ulterior motives? Maybe, it's for Power? Money? Fame?

Even, if we attend community sermons, why do we not directly read the scriptures and discover as well as experience the knowledge ourselves? Why should we be only at the mercy of other people's interpretation and blindly follow their directions? And in the process harm ourselves more than receive any benefit! Religion is man-made, but the universe is God-made. To experience God is to experience the universe as one, and that is the essence of spirituality. It is the restricted, finite, adulterated, and impure interpretation of religious scriptures that makes man distance from another in name of religion.

We may profess religion but we are not spiritual, if we condemn or look down upon another person from a different faith.

To experience spirituality we have to experience a feeling of unity and not just read and memorise scriptures.

It is not a thought, it is a feeling. A good feeling of being one with our Creator and its wonderful creation.

It is important to discuss and clarify as to what man creates and what God creates. Not uncommonly people will argue, "How come God allows so much suffering?" Well, the suffering is created by man, his mind, and his *karmic* debts (reactions of the universe to his negative thoughts, words or actions over a period of time). God only created the universe and sustains it. And in that package, he also created humans and gave them a mind to allow the spirit to operate the body. However, the free will of man gave him the freedom to undertake all kinds of unrighteous actions. The result is a mess today, including a division in humanity based on perceived religions that have been made by humans, not God.

A human society that has highly developed material and spiritual resources, and a complex cultural, political, and legal organisation; an advanced state in social development. And even in that, it is apparent as we scan history of mankind that in more than one ways all the realisations are connected. Judaism, Christianity, and Islam came from the same lineage of Abraham geographically located in the Levant region.

Similarly, Hinduism, Buddhism, and Sikhism are all off-shoots of the Indus Valley civilisation. There are speculations that the Indus Valley settlement may have been preceded by a civilisation that might have had roots in the Levant due to migration of civilisations. Indeed, are we all then not from the same origin? And then has not the same Universal Power created and sustained us? Then how can we assign that Universal Power a title under "Judaism" or "Christianity" or "Hinduism" or "Islam" or "Buddhism" or "Sikhism" or any other religion?

The bottom line is that all humans are embodied souls, connected to each other by our common origin and source of life. This truth becomes apparent as soon as we become soul-conscious. And when our soul connects with the omnipresent power of the universe, in that consciousness we perceive the only real emotion that our soul needs to be satisfied:

Love- a feeling our higher-self experiences on connecting with its universal roots.

When our self finds its roots, our life gives us fruits!

And yet there is such a simple solution for this existence in infinite and immortal bliss: *BE ONE*! That is the recipe for happy and successful life. Many ancient texts have survived thousands of years to tell us the same truth...

.~.

Additional Universal Wisdom for Chapter 7

Old Testament:

Hebrews 10:24

"And let us consider how to stir-up one another to love and good works".

Bhagavad Gita:

Chapter 4, Verse 35

"And when you have thus learned the truth, you will know that all living beings are but part of Me—and that they are in Me, and are Mine."

Chapter 5, Verse 19.

"Those whose minds are established in sameness and equanimity have already conquered the conditions of birth and death."

Chapter 6, Verse 8.

"A person is said to be established in self-realisation and is called a yogi (in union) when he is fully satisfied by virtue of acquired knowledge and realisation. Such a person is situated in transcendence and is self-controlled. He sees everything—whether it be pebbles, stones or gold—as the same."

New Testament Bible:

1 Peter 3:8

"Finally, be ye all of one mind, having compassion one of another, love as brethren, be pitiful, be courteous".

John 15:12

"This is my commandment, that ye love one another, as I have loved you."

Colossians 3:14

"And over all these virtues put on love, which binds them all together in perfect unity."

Qur'an:

Surat 'Âli `Imrân [3:103]:

"And hold firmly to the rope of Allah all together and do not become divided. And remember the favour of Allah upon you - when you were enemies and He brought your hearts together and you became, by His favour, brothers. And you were on the edge of a pit of the Fire, and He saved you from it. Thus, does Allah make clear to you His verses that you may be guided?"

Surat Ash-Shûraá [42:13]:

"He has ordained for you of religion what He enjoined upon Noah and that which we have revealed to you, [O Muhammad], and what we enjoined upon Abraham and Moses and Jesus—to establish the religion and not be divided therein. Difficult for those who associate others with Allah is that to which you invite them. Allah chooses for Himself whom He wills and guides to Himself whoever turns back [to Him]."

Buddha:

"He who experiences the unity of life sees his own Self in all beings, and all beings in his own Self, and looks on everything with an impartial eye."

Guru Granth Sahib:

Page 421:

"They have no doubt or sense of separation — their tongues taste the divine taste"

.~.

Mayan Monuments Reaching up to Heaven!

When a state of peace and bliss will abound in each of us, we will bring back Paradise on Earth!

And it starts with a simple impersonal realisation of the personal self.

Because when we transcend our finite noisy minds to an infinite space of peace and joy we can perceive our divine existence, abounding in love and respect for self and others!

8

Bringing Back Paradise

There is a story about a very aggressive and restless emperor, who wanted to conquer the whole world. He went around violently overtaking all his neighbouring countries to feel important, powerful, popular, and to increase his possessions. In this insane frenzy, he happened to visit India and during one of his crusades he saw a saint silently and peacefully meditating amidst chaos. He was perplexed with the serene calmness, peace and bliss that the saint exuded.

After the emperor had conquered that city, he sent his troops to ask the saint to join him in his journey. The saint replied to the emperor's troops that he was not interested and was happy where he was. The emperor was angry and asked his troops to demand him to join them. To this request again the saint politely declined. By now the emperor was furious and sent his army to demand him to join him with the stern words, "Since the emperor is the master of the land after his conquest, the saint is his slave and has to comply." To this the saint replied, "Not really. Actually, the emperor is the slave of my slave." When the army chief demanded an apology, the saint explained, "I have conquered my mind and its anger, so I am the master of Anger. The emperor is enslaved by Anger, of which I am the master. So, I am the master of the emperor's master. In essence, the emperor is the slave of my slave!." While the saint stayed peacefully at his residence, the emperor returned to his country, victorious in war but defeated in spirit and succumbed to an illness and died young shortly thereafter.

What the story exemplifies is that unless we master our minds, we are slaves to all its vices (lust, anger, greed, attachment, pride) as also to its weaknesses (laziness, deceit, jealousy, blame, grudges). All these are the manifestations of the ego-driven emotional mind, the "I" and "Me" mind. As soon as we realise that *WE* are much more than this ego-driven mind, our intelligence, pure consciousness, and soul driven by the spirit of the universe become accessible to us in their entirety and purity. It is as if we have been released from a prison: a dark, dingy, stifling, restricting, limiting, fear inducing, doubting, critical, discriminating, non-accepting, hateful, jealous and unforgiving surrounding.

Our ego-centric minds make us believe that these emotions are essential for our survival when actually these are the vices in our minds which shroud our true selves and destroy our peace and joy. These negative emotions torment us and make us incapable of experiencing any enjoyment.

Lord Buddha put it very appropriately:

"Holding on to anger is like grasping a hot coal with the intent of throwing it at someone else; you are the one who gets burned.

You will not be punished for your anger, you will be punished by it."

— Buddha

In a state where the awareness is liberated from the thoughts of mind-driven emotions that keep us wrapped up in a pseudo-world of ego-perceived anger, hate, jealousy, lust, greed, pride, deceit, and judgment, one finds peace, wisdom, and joy. And in that state everything will appear fresh, clear, and complete. Learning, performance, confidence, and gentleness will flow uninhibited, and everything will appear easily possible.

As a wise saint has appropriately said:

"Absolve and rise above the dualities of emotions."

I am reminded of the school prayer we used to say almost every day in our morning school assembly, written by Sir Rabindranath Tagore (1861-1941), a philosopher and poet from India who won the Nobel Prize in Literature in 1913:

"Where the Mind is without fear,

and the head is held high.

Where knowledge is free

Where the world has not been broken up into fragments by narrow domestic walls.

Where words come out from the depth of truth,

Where tireless striving stretches its arms towards perfection.

Where the clear stream of reason has not lost its way

into the dreary desert sand of dead habit.

Where the Mind is led forward by thee

Into ever-widening thought and action

Into that heaven of freedom, my Father,

Let my country awake."

This intended beautiful world described above, a reflection of paradise, is possible if the sum total of human consciousness simply becomes and lives through their pure and true self. When each of us drops the shroud of the evil, engulfing ego-driven emotional mind, the collective net result is a pure symbiotic society full of love and appreciation. Compassion and the desire to love, respect, and help all those around us as we feel a belonging to each other becomes our inherent nature.

Often in mathematics one way to ensure that the answer is correct is to apply the deduced answer to the original equation and see if it holds true. What examples do we have to uphold the possibility of bringing Paradise on Earth? What promising souls over the centuries have set examples before us to dream of such an existence? And what philosophies and beliefs have they left for us to follow? Here, are some examples that come to my mind.

.~.

Christianity

When we hear of amazing revelations about our universal connections with the almighty powers, we often doubt them and wonder if these are stories of fiction. As time fades away, the immediate memories of amazing events fade away as well. In later generations, people question the truth of these almost miraculous and what appears to be mystical experiences. And we continue to live in our mind-created, stifling existence of disbelief. Aware that this was a strong possibility, Lord Jesus Christ from Nazareth, in the Levant prepared the world of the future to hear and see the powers that he was going to reveal through his faith and love in the Supreme Power, whom he referred to as 'Father' (what else will be more appropriate to call our creator and sustainer)! Therefore, he handpicked twelve Apostles, who were going to bear testimony to these miracles and spread the truth about our true identity.

It was only to be that the whole world would notice when a supernatural soul in human form would display supernatural powers and perform humanly impossible deeds such as raising the dead and curing the crippled and blind. This revolutionary event of recent times (merely about two thousand years ago compared to the billions of years of existence of the universe) has shaken mankind to an immense degree and has been noted by all.

Historians, spiritualists, politicians, as well as the masses have been affected to such an extent that his birth is taken as a symbol of the start of a new world. The entire history of human kind has been separated into B.C. (Before Christ) and A.D. (After Dominion). One third of the world accepted his teachings and became Christians". And through his life and teachings, this simple, loving, caring, and truthful spirit (*Lord Jesus*) gave us the most important message that we need. He put the entire wisdom of the world in one word: *LOVE!* He compressed all the commandments of the past into just two commandments:

"Love the Lord your God with all your heart and with all your soul and with all your mind. This is the first and greatest commandment. And the second is like it: Love your neighbour as yourself. All the Law and the Prophets hang on these two commandments."

What *Jesus Christ* gave us is a priceless understanding of how to live life. *Love* may be a simple word but has within it the two positive emotions of the seven basic ones our mind tosses us through. These are the emotions of joy and acceptance (others being fear, sadness, disgust, surprise etc.). In the presence of this emotion, all other negative emotions are destroyed. It is an antidote to all the evils because with love for the Creator comes faith, love, and peace in our souls. We lose fear and doubt. True wisdom and courage for righteous action follow. And when we have received all these and apply it to our Creator's creation, we are united with everyone and everything around us. "*We become one*".

.~.

Hinduism

As the Indus Valley civilisation spread further south in Asia to the land currently known as central India, a child was born to a couple imprisoned by the wife's evil brother, who had received prediction that his superhuman nephew would be responsible for his death. All the children born to the couple were killed immediately after their birth. An immaculate conception by the wife, Devki, resulted in the birth of *Lord Krishna* about 3000 B.C. At that time, the guards fell asleep and the prison doors miraculously opened. The father, Vasudev, transported the child to his friend's home for safe-keeping and brought back their friend's daughter. Krishna showed Godly traits performing miracles even as a child and continued to give wisdom and strength to the world around him as he grew up. In the most revered Hindu text, he gives amazing wisdom to a distressed relative and disciple in the middle of a battlefield. This narration is recorded in the *Bhagavad Gita* (Song of God), consisting of about seven hundred verses. It lays the entire gamut of potential ways a human can live in peace and bliss. Predominantly, it talks about attaining this state by uniting with the Supreme Power in a method referred to as "*Yoga*." The four-fold path for obtaining this was delineated by him so that each person may adopt the path accordingly:

Jnana Yoga - (Knowledge Path),

Karam Yoga - (Action Path),

Dhyan Yoga - (Meditation and Focus Path), and

Bhakti Yoga - (Love and Devotion Path).

These four paths cover all different avenues to calm the mind and make it steadfast. If we closely observe our mind, we notice that it acts like a monkey jumping all over with darting thoughts all the time. To *be one* in time and space with total alliance of body, mind and soul is the most crucial undertaking in life. One has to unite within first before seeking any other relationship including union with the Supreme Power. And each of the above mentioned paths is intended to help unite (*yoga*) the self and supreme. If one looks carefully at each of the prevailing religions and spiritual realisations, it appears that they are based on predominantly on one of these paths.

The simpler the spiritual journey and easier the path, the more effective and guaranteed are the results. That is why different paths suit different people. But the *NET RESULT* is the *MOST IMPORTANT* aspect of following any religion or spiritual realisation, and that is to reach the state of *YOGA, which means "union."* This refers to union with self (soul) and the powers of the universe (supreme) and surroundings (synchronisation or synergy). *Lord Krishna* emphasises all of this in his message to the world through his dialogue with Arjuna in a battlefield, which in some ways symbolises the battlefield in our own minds. The true and lasting peace and freedom can only be obtained by realisation of our higher selves and uniting them with their originator, the Super Soul, the Creator and Sustainer of the universe. This unity, according to him, can be most easily and permanently achieved by the path of *Bhakti Yoga (Devotion and Love)*. This is not unlike what Jesus Christ talked about three thousand years later.

Another revered history prominent in Hindu scriptures and of immense significance is the life of Lord Rama, considered as a Supreme being. About seven thousand years ago, probably in the year 5000 B.C., walked on earth a soul that the Hindus talk about to date and perceive him as God-like. *Lord Rama* was the eldest son of the powerful King Dasarath, who had three wives and four sons. As *Lord Rama* was growing, he demonstrated many soul-conscious traits such as complete honesty, steadfast mind, unfaltering wisdom, courage, and complete devotion and obedience in his relationships.

When it came time for him to become king as his father grew old, his step-mother objected and found excuse to send him to the forest for fourteen years. Even this challenge, he bore without complaining, and in the hardship came with him his loving wife Sita to serve him and his younger brother Lakshman to protect them, demonstrating to the world the familial responsibilities. In the forest his wife was abducted by an evil and greedy king, Ravana. In the symbolic war between *Rama* and Ravana, *Rama* destroys the evil king and unites again with his wife. The life story of *Rama* depicts the importance of truth, righteousness, and courage to be victorious in life. Sometimes the evil is within our minds in the form of greed, lust, and conceit. But our true identity is pure and honest in the form of the soul, which, when connected with the powers of the universe, can overcome all our weaknesses. The important thing is to be aware what is our weakness and what is our true strength, know what is vice and what is virtue, and strive to live a life of *righteousness* without fear.

Rich in its spiritual conceptualisation, Hinduism also agrees that the universe exists because of the omnipresent and all-powerful force referred to as *Bhagwan*. The universe operates through the trinity of the creator (referred to as *Brahma)*, sustainer (*Vishnu*) and destroyer of evil (*Mahesh or Shiv*). Their utterance of *"Aum Tat Sat"* is not unlike the concept of the Father, Son, and Holy Spirit in Christianity. In some ways, it also is symbolic of mind, body, and spirit.

.~.

Judaism

Also referred to as *Moshe Rabbenu* in Hebrew, Moses is considered to be the author of Torah, the religious script for Jews. As a young man, he was angered to see unfair beatings of Israelite, which caused him to kill the abuser and then flee. At a time of prayer, he received the "Ten Commandments" on Mount Sinai, and empowered by the wisdom and courage, he led the Israelites to safety from the Egyptians.

Those *Ten Commandments* were incorporated in the Jewish beliefs, which include the following:

- Honour God,
- Do not use any graven images for God,
- Respect your parents,
- Do not take God's name in vain,
- Observe the Sabbath day (holy day once a week),
- Do not engage in adultery,
- Do not steal,
- Do not murder,
- Do not bear false testimony and
- Do not covet the neighbour's possessions.

These words of wisdom serve as a simple recipe for a successful and happy life. This is similar to the wisdom perceived by other shining stars who have walked as humans, exemplifying righteousness and belief in the higher power. It is living a life of *Compassion*.

.~.

Buddhism

When a man was born into an extremely privileged family, blessed with the most desirous materialistic riches and endowed with fame and power, decided to give up everything in quest for his true identity, the whole world took note.

Siddharta Gautama in the fifth century searched for the wisdom to guide him to a life of peace and joy, to reach a steadfast mind, which would not be disturbed by the waxing and waning nature of physical and mental perturbations. And after years of deep meditation, he reached that desirable state of unfaltering bliss. He rolled out the wisdom of his realisations into the Four Noble Truths, Eight-fold Path, Three Jewels, and Five Precepts. Through these he helped people realise the achievement of the Four Immeasurable, comprising unconditional love, compassion, sympathetic joy (happiness in other's happiness), and equanimity (clear-minded, tranquil state of mind). His practical step-by-step notes encouraged people to follow the Eight-fold Path:

1. Right View,
2. Right Thought,
3. Right Speech,
4. Right Action,
5. Right Livelihood,
6. Right Effort,
7. Right Mindfulness and
8. Right Concentration.

To achieve and retain this state, he encouraged adhering to the Three Jewels, which are *Buddha* (wisdom of the Enlightened One), *Dharma* (laws of nature), and *Sangha* (congregation of similar followers).

It is remarkable that what he taught and preached was not different from what other spiritually enlightened humans have noted: a righteous path, wisdom from one who has been liberated, and company of like-minded individuals to realise *love* and happiness!

Islam

Prophet Muhammad, from the Middle East around A.D. 570, was known to retreat in solitude in caves and pray many times and is said to have received the word of God by Archangel Gabriel. The knowledge he received was compiled into the Islamic holy text, the *Qur'an.* Elaborate in giving instructions for ethical principles, and code of conduct, the *Qur'an* along with *Hadees* (quotes by Muhammad) are considered crucial Islamic scriptures. The religion endorses the application of Five Pillars in practice for the Muslims, namely:

- *Shahadah* (testimony to oneness of Allah and Prophethood of Mohammad),
- *Salat* (daily Prayers),
- *Zakat* (charity),
- *Sawm* (fasting), and
- *Hajj* (pilgrimage to the Holy City of Mecca).

At the core of the religion the basic principle and essence is to *love* God and serve his purpose righteously.

.~.

Sikhism

In the fifteenth century in northern India was born an amazing child to a God-fearing couple. This child was predicted to be a future saint. This childhood was also influenced by the governing of Mogul Empire ruling during those times in India. The pull and push of different religions did not confuse the pure heart of this intelligent child, who learnt different languages to comprehend the scriptures of different religions.

Guru Nanak realised and awakened to the ultimate truth of: "*Ik Onkaar. Sat Sri Akaal*" which means: *"There is only One Sound which reigns, and that is TRUTH."* He urged those who sought his wisdom to pursue that truth by using the Three Pillars:

- *Simran* (meditation on God by recitation of God's name),
- *Kirat Karni* (truthful and earnest living with God's blessings) and
- *Vand Chakko* (share with Community).

The entire Holy Scripture of *Guru Granth Sahib* speaks of praise and *Love* for God and urges to truthfully surrender to his will.

.~.

Other Philosophies

The list is long, but the concept is similar: righteousness, good over evil, right over wrong, peace over distress. Be it the *Zoroastrian* religion started by *Zoroaster* or *Jainism* by *Mahavira* or *Bahai* by *Bahaullah*, the message is to help a person find a higher ground to exist in an unselfish manner.

When different religions teach the same truth, it is not surprising to see faiths like the *Bahai* religion to emerge and endorse the unity of religion and human kind under one concept of God.

Sai Baba of Shirdi is a beautiful personification of this realisation. Described by his followers as a "God-like" Enlightened Soul, he walked on earth as recently as 1918. He lovingly taught from Christianity, Hinduism, and Islam, and is known to often remark "*Sabka Malik Ek*" (one God is master of all). He emphasised the need to have a relationship with God rather than boast about belonging to any religion.

.~.

And then our earth has seen other great souls who have had similar realisations. The list is never-ending and the common thread in all their messages is to follow a righteous path dictated by truth, love, and compassion.

Confucius:

"Never impose on others what you would not choose for yourself."

Pythagoras:

"To recognise the Divine Essence — this is the highest purpose of soul, sent by the Creator to the Earth!"

"Friends are companions on a journey, who ought to aid each other to persevere in the road to a happier life."

Aristotle:

"*Love* is composed of a single soul inhabiting two bodies."

Socrates:

"Know thyself"—"We cannot live better than seeking to become better".

Mother Teresa:

"Let us always meet each other with smile, for the smile is the beginning of love."

Martin Luther King:

"Faith must trample under foot, all reason, sense and understanding."

Mahatma Gandhi:

"Where there is love there is life."

Abraham Lincoln:

"To ease another's heartache is to forget one's own."

Dalai Lama:

"Compassion and love are not mere luxuries. As the source both of inner and external peace, they are fundamental to the continued survival of our species."

~

Probably, the most beautiful verse about love, which is desperately needed in our world today, is given in the *Holy Bible*:

New Testəment:

(Corinthians) 13:

"....If I give all I possess to the poor and give over my Body to hardship that I may boast, but do not have love, I gain nothing.

Love is patient, love is kind. It does not envy, it does not boast, it is not proud. It does not dishonour others, it is not self-seeking, it is not easily angered, and it keeps no record of wrongs. Love does not delight in evil but rejoices with the truth. It always protects, always trusts, always hopes, and always perseveres.

...And now these three remain: faith, hope and love. But the greatest of these is love."

In my own opinion, all religions and true philosophies for happiness and success come down to:

Love our Creator, Love his Creation

The true essence of life is to live with love and respect through compassion for everyone including ourselves.

Love is to joyfully accept whatever and however we or another person is and care for another such that their happiness becomes our happiness.

Respect is treating oneself and others with dignity just as we would like to be treated.

In this distressing world, what we urgently need is just that: *Love*! It is worth noting that many of the enlightened souls that have walked on the earth went through a distressful period before seeking higher self-realisation and realising this feeling of love. This is not unlike the flowering of the beautiful lotus in the midst of a swamp. When we are so tormented by the mind that we truly want to lose it, we suddenly come to a stage when we realise that we really do not need it! In fact, we are so much better without it because the true higher self, the soul peeks out of its hidden covers and layers and leads us into a most blissful life full of wisdom. When happiness abounds and success is assured, what else do we need? But considering that eighty-five per cent of the world population is practising religion in one form or another according to the *CIA World* Fact Book 2010, why is our world not looking like paradise already?

Are we all thinking religion and not feeling religion, which is spirituality? Are we all in 'lip service' rather than 'heart service?' Are we using religion for advantage rather than righteousness?

Are we all waiting to go down into the worst state of existence with distress, distrust and destruction before we emerge a new?

.~.

Time Changes Everything Except the Truth.

Each one of us has to first take care of self with full responsibility of our thoughts, words, and actions by aligning ourselves correctly in body, mind, and soul.

Thereafter, it becomes our duty to give this wisdom to those around us without losing our own balance or entangling ourselves with others' progress.

One by one, slowly but surely the world will change...it has to be because we have come to the end of the rope...we have no other choice...

9

Beginning of a New Beginning

The world needs to change, the world has to change, the world has been predicted to change, and the world *will* change. And with it, all its inhabitants have to change from their current state of existence because those who don't will break down, suffer, decay, and perish miserably. The change starts with each one of us because as someone has appropriately said, *"Nothing in my life will change unless I do."*

What we perceive as 'I' needs to be a realisation of a complete human entity packaged as body-mind-soul. However, the deep realisation that the immortal soul is the true originator of our being allows us to experience a simple switch: from untrue to true identity. We then go from a body- and mind-conscious entity to a soul-realised life force. We become equipped with the knowledge that our existence is because our soul sought to experience the world and took up a body for that purpose. And that the mind is merely an operating gear. Our true driver, the soul, knows what to do and where to go and how to do righteously. In its pure and divine state, uncontaminated by the ego-driven mind's interpretation, it has the true wisdom and strength to function in its and the world's best interest. What is amazing is that it is pre-packaged with the *GPS: God Protective/Providing Services!* When we get connected to the universe we are guided and recharged with the everlasting energy source. This source teaches us to be like it; ever-flexible and adapting life forces that stay unperturbed, happy and content in any situation synchronised with everything around us.

Just like each of the hundred trillion cells in the body is programmed to carry out their specific functions without any reminders, we carry in us the wisdom and courage to live a happy and successful life. Similar to the fact that the cells are pre-packaged with a central DNA in its nucleus, the soul comes pre-packaged with its set of inner wisdom. And just like the cell continues to thrive with nourishment of food and oxygen, the soul continues to guide the functioning of the body and intelligence wondrously when connected with the energising acceptance of the universe. From the smallest to the largest structures in the universe, like the planets and stars, the harmonious pre-programmed path of all beings is laid out by the creator of the universe. The synergy between the universe within and without is the recipe of life.

When strong winds gust over a town, the trees that are rigid break while those are ready to bend and be flexible, survive and stay tall, like the palm tree. Similarly, if we are to survive in this torrential change, which has ensued, we have to be flexible and change in according with the law of nature. And that law simply put is "Synchronise." Synchronise with yourself first, then the environment, and all beings around you fully appreciating, and accepting the powers, and laws of the universe. Only in that state, can we truly and deeply enjoy our existence because, it is appreciated by our soul. That is true happiness, the liberation achieved from the torrential torture of the mind.

When each one of us undertakes this in ourselves and in our lives, the entire world is bound to change because the world is nothing but each one of us put together. It is not possible to be in synergy if we exist at only the physical level, because the desires stemming from our sense organs make us selfish and limited in our perception. Even if we rise from the clutches of the lust-laden bodily needs, we cannot rest in peace because now we find ourselves in the clutches of an even greedier and unsteady mind. But when we rest in the naturally peaceful, joyful, and content soul, that is when all of our best attributes arise: purity, truth, wisdom, courage, love, peace, joy and faith. The quiet mind finally perceives the feeling of infinite and eternal bliss. This self-knowledge is considered the most important realisation for humans and is referred to as: "*Prajna*" (Sanskrit word meaning knowledge of self; *pra* means self, *jna* means knowledge). It is awareness of our true identity.

Aristotle, a great philosopher whose wisdom and insights have transcended time and influenced mankind since the third century B.C., has emphatically stated:

"Knowing yourself is the beginning of all wisdom."

"Happiness is the meaning and the purpose of life, the whole aim and end of human existence."

—Aristotle

It is the attainment of this self-knowledge that illuminates our lives and takes us from dark, suffering, distressed, searching entities to enlightened, peaceful, happy, and knowing individuals. The only feeling left and felt at the core of our existence is *Love*. In that feeling of love for all, one has only a single choice, and that is to practise *Compassion*. We start living a life of love and respect. And when we receive this feeling from our higher self and its connections with the Universe, we can then give it to others. We can only give what we have, so unless we experience love and respect, we cannot give it to others. But before we give it to anyone else, we have to begin with ourselves. In the words of the wise:

"But first, and above all, love and respect yourself."

.~.

This realisation has dawned on mankind for centuries, and the greatest souls have declared it uninhibitedly many times: Sophocles, an acclaimed Greek dramatist, who lived about four hundred years before *Christ*, knew the power of this one emotion—love. Psychologists talk about primary emotions that are comprehended by a human: joy, acceptance, fear, surprise, sadness, disgust, and anger. As one can see there are only two positive emotions, while all the others are negative and often torment us by an overactive mind. When these two positive emotions, joy and acceptance, are put together, the resultant emotion is love—a form of secondary emotion. This helps us understand that love is a blended emotion of two very wonderfully comforting feeling within us. Hence, love is an antidote to all the negative energy that can potentially arise within us. In a state of realisation, which may be looked upon as 'realisation' (or the understanding of who I really am), that is the only feeling that remains—unconditional love.

"One word frees us of all the weight and pain of life. The word is love."

— Sophocles

Even in the most amazing life stories of our current times, we have witnessed this realisation being brought to our attention. One such great soul that has illuminated the world is undoubtedly Mother Teresa, who was bestowed with a Noble Peace Prize for her loving devotion to the needy and the poor. Blessed by the Higher Power's guidance early in her life, she has shown us how that one emotion (love) needs to be at the core of every step that we take:

"In this life we cannot do great things. We can only do small things with great love."

— Mother Teresa

Knowing that this is what we are to strive for, we can help promote happiness and bliss in life. And if it is possible with a simple self-realisation, it would be our foolishness to seek any other way of life. In that state of self-realisation, having experienced unconditional love from within ourselves as we connect with the energy of the universe, compassion is irrefutable. Considering that we are all living challenging lives, how can we add to each other's burden when we are our only help?

Sometimes we blame our environment and disruptive elements in our lives for our thoughts and life situation. The fact of the matter is that those individuals also got there because of what they have gone through in life, and sometimes we are responsible for their state! In essence we are caught in a vicious cycle of tormenting each other emotionally and creating monsters in others and ourselves! Where is this to lead all of us? The only hope is for some of us to gain wisdom and then send wisdom to another through actions, practice, teachings, books, audio, TV, internet, or preaching in community gatherings and bring everyone eventually to their birthright! And through this period of transition it would be helpful to remember what Socrates wisely said:

"Be kind, for everyone you meet is fighting a hard battle."

— Socrates

For those of us who are living in a highly intellectual state with overuse of our head instead of the heart (as a physician, scientist and educator, I have been there!). Albert Einstein provides a good role model for understanding this realisation. He is clearly one of the greatest scientists of the past, and his own realisation was:

"I want to know how God created this world. I am not interested in this or that phenomenon, in the spectrum of this or that element.

I want to know God's thoughts. The rest are details."

—Albert Einstein

The genius in that man to prove to us the connection between mass and energy brings great insight into our true state. The triumphant symbolic equation gifted by him to the world further proves his realisation that all matter is related closely to energy and is essentially energy showing itself as mass in motion:

$$e = mc^2$$

If energy is mass in motion, then undeniably we are energy sources. The body itself is lifeless and lacks energy once the life force leaves it, as it is evident in a dead body. The mind also is merely an intellectual entity in the brain. The life force that prevails in us, that energises and keeps our bodies in a living state is the soul. I had the good fortune of witnessing this energy when I undertook a week-long meditation course with Monroe Institute in northern California. On a day, when I decided to practice "mute awake meditation," we were put through a meditative exercise to have an "out-of-body realisation in a lying down posture. Although I had been meditating since 1980, their prompts sent me so deep into the mediation that not only could a part of me see my body lying down lifeless, but that part of me also merged with a warm, golden glow of light and energy that felt so wonderful. On their instructions to return, "I" (the soul) felt totally confused, not knowing for some time who I (the body and mind) was, or where I was! In that amazingly divine experience it occurred to me that:

No one should have the misfortune of departing from the physical form without experiencing being formless! The liberation offered by that realisation will show you the truth.

As a scientist that experience left me completely baffled and somewhat fearful since I could not explain what I had experienced. What was that warm, glowing, golden form that merged with the expanse of another similar, larger form and could perceive the body lying lifeless on the meditating couch? Why was it so peaceful in that warm glow that it merged with that it returned reluctantly almost forgetting who or what it originally was? Was that large expanse of warm glow what we refer to as the Universal Energy?

That dilemma persisted with me for a long time until I decided to know "God," the Universal Power and Energy. I searched the wisdom imparted by "Superhumans" recorded in texts and Holy Scriptures. When their wisdom vibrates with the same frequency as the internal wisdom perceived from the core and depths of our being, truth becomes obvious. And the conclusion is crystal clear to me now: that indeed there is a Universal Power that imparts the energy that creates and sustains all of us. It is in our best interest to accept it. That Power keeps all accounts of positive and negative words and works, and our life will play out now or later according to that equation and balance. It is in our best interest to believe and follow its rules and regulations.

For anyone who still doubts the existence of the omnipresent and all powerful universal power, they need to contemplate on this simple query: From what power does the sun, moon and stars originate? What energy allows plants and trees to bear flowers and fruits? What maintains the flowing rivers, seas and oceans or takes care of the balance between thousands of species? This is just a snap shot of the Universe! *God is true and Almighty!*

'God to me' is:

Giver of destiny as we make our choices with the chances we are given.

It is the Power that created the universe and the Energy that sustains it.

Every moment offers us with chances, and what ensues in our life is the result of our choices.

If those choices are righteous and compassionate with pure intent and consciousness, we can be rest assured that the results will be just a reflection of our choices.

A human may plan life to the tiniest detail, but it will be played out by the equation set forth by the Universal Power. However, one life-time may not be enough to explain questionable occurrences. It is the cyclical stories of a soul that will explain the complete list of actions and results. Many such realisations from wise souls have come forth repeatedly:

"Man proposes, and God disposes."

"Life happens while we plan for it."

This does not mean that we stop planning, but while we plan we have to remember that each moment counts. Only by living in the moment can we do complete justice to life. By being mindful that our true life force is our soul, whose only true need is love, we seek and treasure love rather than materialistic attractions. When we fill ourselves with love, it is only natural to give it to others because we can only share what we possess. Simply by treating everyone compassionately, we can know all the rules of righteousness and live through our higher selves. As aptly put by wise Confucius:

"A superior man is aware of righteousness,

An inferior man is aware of advantage".

— Confucius

It may *appear* that by taking short-cuts and advantages, an individual can flourish quickly, but sooner or later he will have to pay a big price. Each moment of our life is a test that the Higher Power keeps an account of. It is just a matter of time how our lives will show the results of unrighteous action. If we start living each moment guided by the laws of that Higher Power, we are assured peace and joy in our hearts and know that we will be taken care of in all eventualities.

And when we truly know our higher selves and connect with the Higher Power from the heart and soul rather than the mind, we stop seeking materialistic desires because the peace and joy we receive is priceless. We work in and with *righteousness* (also referred to as "*Dharma*" and "Rectitude") with a clear mind and conscience so that we are able to achieve the most privileged positions in the world. All materialistic needs come easily without even asking.

.~.

Another wonderful outcome of living in our higher self is that we are able to have a heightened sense of awareness and insight to know if another being is intending to harm us. Just being in the presence of an "advantage seeking" being, one can perceive the alteration in our blissful energy field. Just like we would not go to a clothing store if we needed grocery, we start seeking the company of those in peace and joy. It is easy then to dissociate and avoid dealings with unrighteousness until such time that we get a better handle on the situation or the other individual elevates to a higher ground. Interestingly, even the *intent* of others becomes clear to the one in "Soul consciousness" irrespective of others words or actions. But even in those circumstances we are able to send them compassion and love and wisdom from far without getting entangled with them or their schemes. In doing so, we retain our peace and joy and show others a path to do the same.

Because of this realisation that eventually each person will pay for their actions, as nothing is hidden from the omnipresent power of the Universe, we can let go of any hurts and wrong-doings by another being! As a result, we liberate ourselves from our own mind tormenting thoughts around past, inappropriate words and actions by other people. In that state of having shed all our hurt feelings, one feels as if we were a caterpillar trapped in a cocoon and have suddenly emerged as a butterfly. The light butterfly feeling like dancing, is the most wondrous perception in the world. I still remember what helped me tremendously was a prayer in the Church one day which talked about:

"Let Go

And Let God....."

And then the wisdom perceived by the higher-self from that of the Universe clarified to me that:

"God or the Universal Power can only do justice if I stop keeping tabs, accounts, thoughts about another person and trying to do justice."

That moment changed my life to this feeling of complete freedom from my mind.

With forgiveness comes freedom, because you allow yourself to forget what does not matter or hold true in the present!

Thoughts of decades of wrong-doing by others, despite my complete love and support towards them, vanished in thin air as if by magic. And unfortunately for the wrong doers, their world came crashing in ways humanly unimaginable. They received such severe consequence for their unrighteousness that I was moved to the point of praying for them. But I remembered a clear sermon, *"Once you have Let Go, now you Let God"*. And when I felt we needed to forgive and not punish, I realised from the inner wisdom, "*Everyone must pay for their deeds, forgiveness from God only comes with repentance. It is not your problem anymore so do not get entangled"*. Indeed once we release all thoughts of another person's wrong-doing, their own *"karmic* debts" are able to give them the consequences to show them right from wrong. The higher power sees to it that eventually all of us learn to stand straight as candles burning bright in front of the Sun, rather than tilt and burn other! Those that do tilt and burn others soon fall and burn themselves out, once the supporting candles give way: i.e., they let go completely!

Every thought word and action is accounted for in the Universe. It is just a matter of time when the results will manifest.

.~.

It is of paramount importance to realise that to be in this state of bliss, one has to be completely pure in their intent. Because intent is the determinant of the seeds (thought, word, and action) that one sows. And with a pure intent, one lives from the core of one's existence, the soul. Therein is endowed the clear blueprint of righteousness: truth, justice, and compassion without any thoughts of greed or advantage-seeking schemes. Because, in that state, we are directly connected with the powers and energy of the universe. When we believe in the powers of Universe, Supreme, God, it means:

"Believe in God: Be like God and live like God"

To be and live like God we need to know what God is like. And God is:

God is truthful, loving, wise, strong, faithful, just, forgiving, merciful, peaceful, joyful, fearless, and pure and everything that is righteous and compassionate.

If nothing else, God can be considered as a great equaliser. In mathematics, justification of balance in an equation comes from the conceptual understanding of one being equal to another if they both are equal to one.

Hence, $A=B \text{ if } A=G \text{ and } B=G.$

For a balanced society, there has to be equilibrium among its members, otherwise the bigger fish will eat the smaller, and the smaller will consume the smallest. Eventually, there will be no small fishes left. From lack of food, even the big fish will die. And on top of that, we are humans, so how can we "eat up" our own species?! Simply by each of us trying to be like God (G) in the above equation, we can be at a mutually acceptable platform, conducive to the growth and achievement of full potential of each and every being. Even if we cannot extend this generosity to everyone we encounter initially, we are required to do so to those souls that fate has put in our direct lives such as parents, spouses, children. If each one wants to live one's own way, chaos and conflict is assured. However, if each of the members in a family and then community and then world seeks the true wisdom of God and starts living in "heart service," we will be partying everyday!

Understanding that each of us is equivalent to an omnipresent power and, through that, equivalent to each other, there is suddenly a sense of peace that takes away the stress and compulsion to compete and fight for every opportunity, achievement, every moment of our lives. This is what we are hearing even from even psychologists, business planners, successful personalities, entrepreneurs, and highly educated masters. It is called:

"Win-win".

You win, I win, we all win...the opportunities are plenty for all of us, and the potential for infinite happiness is there for all of us; we just have to unite. Wish for others what you want for yourself. You can see that any other way is "lose-lose." This is because every action has an equal and opposite reaction. Meaning if the other person loses *because of your misdeed, the "karmic" effect of those deeds falls upon you.* So even if you supposedly win in an unrighteous manner, you eventually lose. On the other hand, if you are putting in your action and the other is doing the same and in all fairness you are to win because you have worked harder at it, then your win is justified and his loss is also justified. If this justified result of two actions is a "Win-win" for both, meaning none of you carry any *karmic* debts as you both have acted to the best of your capabilities and accepted the just result. With such an attitude, one is happy even in the midst of one's so-called loss, since we are aware that it is only a *perceived* loss by our egoistic mind. On the other hand, when we are soul-conscious, even if an opponent performer wins, we can feel joy, satisfied with the perspective that it is well-deserved and that we participated in another person's win. Their win becomes our win.

.~.

This does not mean that despite your whole-hearted pure and sincere intent, words and action, if the other person shows no sign of honest and well meaning interaction, that we have to succumb ourselves repeatedly to harmful ways of another individual. It merely implies that you need to dissociate from that person until that person demonstrates the true wisdom of life and adds to your positive energy. You can only send them wisdom by giving or directing towards them the source of your enlightenment.

A simple rule I follow is a "three strike and dissociate plan". If a person has repeatedly demonstrated that they are uncompassionate and insensitive and live out of their lower self-seeking advantage, being untruthful and hurtful, we need to dissociate.

The most essential requirement for any individual is to first and foremost give ourselves love and respect and distance from those elements which do not allow us to be one with ourselves.

It is better to let the others grow in their realisation and get to a higher understanding before we waste more time, effort, energy and resources and drain ourselves. Because:

First time error is a mistake

Second time it is a blunder

Third time it is a tragedy

And, thereafter it is hell!

Sometime even an animal can show us that path of living in the moment with peace and joy by showering us with unconditional love. This would be apparent to those who have had a pet. The faithful loving and caring attention that pets can show and playfully enjoy each moment with their masters can become model behaviour for us. But if you have to dissociate from a relationship because of the foolishness and impure intent of another person, *do not c*arry the baggage of his or her intent, words, or actions in your mind. Free yourself of any load that another being may have intended for you because it is that person's *karma* or negative energy that will being wrath on him or her, not you.

Don't try to figure out the past, forget it!

Don't drag the garbage bag, just drop it!

By holding on to those wrong-doings in your mind, you prevent that person from receiving what he or she deserves to get to help them set their thinking straight. When you let go of another person's words or action in your mind, you liberate yourself from holding yourself accountable to their deeds. Then, they receive what their words and actions will bear as fruits. But most importantly, y*ou have to let go and let God!* And everyone eventually learns the most important lesson in life:

As you sow, so you reap,
Intent will determine hug or blow!

In a regulated manner by serving justice, the Universe sincerely intends to have everyone go through the appropriate experience to come to a realisation that the only way to live is "Win-win". It is as if a drama is being played out on Earth, so that each soul can learn the lesson of life—that one can be in peace and joy and love by getting and giving just those. And if they cannot find that in their friends or relationships, there are people living out of their higher selves who can show them that.

Often, we are confused as to which religious background and scriptures are the best options for our growth or to find compassionate people. As I have discovered, all religions and scriptures have the same power. However, although it does not matter which religion one follows: Christianity, Hinduism, Judaism, Sikhism, Islam; it is important to not leave the scriptures to the interpretation of others. It is essential to know, understand, feel and experience the wisdom yourself.

Spirituality is the study of the spirit and it is only possible if you experience your own spirit, no one else can do it for you.

If you subject yourself to only other people's interpretations, you do not know if they are in *"lip service" or "heart service."* The difference between the two is that some people talk about religion for their own fame and glory; that is *lip service.* These people are still operating from their *inferior selves driven by their ego-minds, and they look for advantage.* But seek the company of those who know, feel, and stay connected with the energy of the universe and show you how to do the same; that is *heart service.* These people are fully conscious, alert and awake operating from their *superior selves driven by their souls," and they follow path of truth and display compassion.* They have nothing but *your* and the community's best interest in mind, not their own hidden agenda. *They know and practice righteousness rather than misusing their power to seek advantage.* They feel your pain and want to help you instead of using and abusing your trust, helplessness, and service for their advantage.

The beings endowed with heart service are aware that the Higher Power or Supreme Power, or Almighty, or God, or Father in Heaven, or *Allah,* or *Bhagwan,* or *Ik Onkaar* are names used to describe the same Creator and Sustaining Power and Energy of the universe. What each of these is referring to is "Infinite and Eternal Universal Energy full of love, wisdom, and courage"

Just like you may be called by your first name or last name or nick name or different names such as "Father, Son, Brother, Husband" or "Mother, Daughter, Sister, Wife" by different relatives, that does not mean we are so many different people! We are the same one, just different names.

Similarly, depending upon the realisations by different groups of people and civilisations in different times in history and regions in the world, the name for that All Powerful Life-Force Sustainer has received different names. And different philosophies and religions provide us with recipes of life to stay connected with that Energy for our own good.

Following an inspiring lecture delivered at Saint Louis University by a professor from Boston College, a person from the audience asked him, in what light he saw other faiths now that he was older. The distinguished speaker paused for a moment, and in a very humble and sincere manner he replied, "Earlier I used to think when I met people of other religions that I have something that they don't. Now, I feel that they probably have something that I don't." It cannot be said with more honesty and sincerity than that! I could see that this man had crossed the boundaries that man creates around himself to stifle his connections with the universe. He had broken the chains of interpretation that we force on our community. He is truly liberated and free to experience the presence of the divine power in all its manifestations. For as a distinguished former US president Abraham Lincoln said:

"When I do good, I feel good.

When I do bad, I feel bad.

And that's my religion."

—Abraham Lincoln

.~.

I consider myself very fortunate to be with the parents, who were soul-conscious and never objected to my interest in other religions as long as I was imbibing truth, compassion and were on the path of righteousness. This has allowed me to enjoy and foster the best aspects and emphasis of each of them: love and compassion in Christianity; self-analysis, self-control and paths of union with the Supreme in Hinduism; discipline, such as praying many times a day, fasting, and pilgrimage of Islam; self-responsibility and focus in Buddhism; complete surrender to and gratitude for God in Sikhism; peace and respect for my time in prayers with Judaism. And Righteousness reinforced by All Religions. I would not want to miss any of these in my search for me and my Creator's true identities. As I blend all these beautiful recipes in my life, it becomes an amazingly flavourful and rich experience.

However, the author is not suggesting or enforcing such a life-style, just expressing amazement at the beauty in the length, breadth, and depth of human realisations. It is only through the eyes of the soul that one perceives the unity in all religions, rising above the limitations of the mind.

With this blissful experience, the realisation dawns

that while the wisdom of the soul tends to unite,

thoughts in the mind, influenced by ego, divide,

and with division, we lose our strength inside and out.

When the prevailing force of comprehension in the world is mind, the earth and world becomes divided. Unfortunately, the limited, finite mind restricts full understanding of what we are in totality, given the constraints and boundaries of Ego.

If man were to live on Ocean, Air or Sky, he would use means to even divide them!

...Man tries to divide the universe and its power in order to make himself feel important, but in the process, he destroys

the sacredness, divinity, and purity of this blissful journey called life!

The greatest evil responsible for disturbing his peace is within his own mind: his Ego.

For a soul uncontaminated by an impure mind, all surroundings become Church, Mosque, Temple, Synagogue, Gurudwara...

And in that state our lives become worship...led by truth and love...giving us contentment and happiness.

This is a far cry from today's existing ego-driven thinking of our communities. Even when we do have materialistic gains, we are not content, or we even suffer from fear, insecurities, and resultant depression and anxiety. The trips to holy places become meaningless as ignorance only reinforces evil within us and breeds hate and restlessness. Such an existence threatens the survival of the human race in its totality. No other species eats one of its own kinds, but man is doing just that.

And all that for what? For surviving few extra years in the bodily living with guilt and distress? Wars are a clear indication of the destruction man intends for his own species.

A wise person has appropriately said, *"The best way to stop a war is to never start it."* Confucius, a wise philosopher who lived in the 6th century BC observed very appropriately that "Life is really simple, but we deliberately insist on making it complicated." He recognised that in this complicated state:

"He, who is not contented with what he has, he would not be contented with what he would like to have."

— Confucius

Unknowingly, we may have committed blunders ourselves. Because of this we may be bearing consequences that are causing us to suffer from disease. Science is recognising more and more that the mental state of a person can alter chemicals in the body as hormones or neurotransmitters. These act on the DNA (Deoxyribose Nucleic Acid: the core message system in the nucleus within each cell of the body), and turn on the production of harmful peptides in our cells, which start producing disease instead of health.

However, by simply living in the higher, superior self-connected with the Universal Power, one can turn off this switch of self-destruction and start healing. In the Hindu scriptures this is referred to as "*Sahaja Avastha*" and "*Sahaja Samadhi*" or which means "State of Ease" the opposite of "Dis-Ease"! And with continuous practice one can be in this state all the time. Imagine a world full of individuals practicing such a life for their own and others' well-being!!

And once we have come to the simple realisation of how we can always be in a state of peace and joy by being here and now in body, mind and soul, we will be naturally led to seek it again and again.

The speed of the progress does not matter; it is just a matter of time when we will start living in that state all the time.

If you have a disease state for which you are under medical therapy and yet not making progress as you should, there is probably a hindrance to the flow of positive energy around you. Firstly, surround yourself with positive energy in clean and pleasing surroundings with people who are joyous and peaceful. Seek wisdom on understanding yourself and the energy and power of the universe. That infinite, eternal power can connect with you and give you grace to bring you back from disease to "ease." Grace is a favour extended to you despite what your past attitude, intent, thoughts, words, and actions have been. But it requires existing in a new and transformed state of purity. For our own good, the simplest way to enter this state of ease is a two-step process prompted by two simple realisations:

1. *We need the Universal Power and Energy to heal completely.*

2. *For the powers of the universe to grace us with that privilege, we need to show repentance and surrender.*

Repentance is the realisation of what you did wrong or unrighteous (hate, jealousy, harm, greed, lust, violence, hurt another by intent, thought, word, or deed). *AND* a promise to never do it again, because the Universal Power wants the assurance from you that once it returns you to help, you will not misuse your energy.

Surrender is to submit completely to the will of the Divine, and it has to be complete in body, mind, and soul. This means walking, talking, thinking, doing, and feeling as shown by the Universal Power. These directions are revealed to us by our inner-wisdom and superimposed by scriptures. In essence being faithful and loving towards the Universal Power or God from your entire being.

As the world of humans today has evolved to a life-style and mind-set of living in extreme stress, we all yearn for a new way of existing. In the words of the maxim: *"For us to change, we have to be sick and tired of being sick and tired!"*

And as we implement the simple philosophy of living in our higher selves with universal wisdom, we start healing and begin life anew:

Life is a journey of the soul on earth embodied in physical form. Its main purpose is to love, enjoy, and learn.

The path is a two-way street, so you get what you give, and you give what you get.

One cannot give without receiving and neither can one receive without giving!

And once you start living from your soul instead of your mind, the feeling of love guides you to find love and share love.

.~.

Additional Universal Wisdom for Chapter 9

Old Testament Bible:

Isaiah [42:5-7]

"This is what God the LORD says, He who created the heavens and stretched them out, who spread out the earth and all that comes out of it, who gives breath to its people, and life to those who walk on it: "I, the LORD, have called you in righteousness; I will take hold of your hand. I will keep you and will make you to be a covenant for the people and a light for the Gentiles, to open eyes that are blind, to free captives from prison and to release from the dungeon those who sit in darkness."

Psalm 36:6

"Your righteousness is like the mighty mountains, your justice like the great deep. O LORD, you preserve both man and beast."

Jeremiah 9:23-24

"This is what the LORD says: "Let not the wise man boast of his wisdom or the strong man boast of his strength or the rich man boast of his riches, but let him who boasts about this: that he understands and knows me, that I am the LORD, who exercises kindness, justice and righteousness on earth, for in these I delight," declares the LORD."

Exodus 15:26

He said, "If you listen carefully to the voice of the LORD your God and do what is right in his eyes, if you pay attention to his commands and keep all his decrees, I will not bring on you any of the diseases I brought on the Egyptians, for I am the LORD, who heals you."

Psalm 107:19-21

"Then they cried to the LORD in their trouble, and He saved them from their distress. He sent forth his word and healed them; He rescued them from the grave. Let them give thanks to the LORD for His unfailing love and His wonderful deeds for men."

Bhagavad Gita:

Chapter 4, Verse 38.

"In this world, there is nothing so sublime and pure as transcendental knowledge. Such knowledge is the mature fruit of all mysticism. And one who has achieved this enjoys the self with himself in due course of time."

Chapter 4, Verse 39.

"A faithful man who is absorbed in transcendental knowledge and who subdues his senses quickly attains the supreme spiritual peace."

Chapter 6:25-27

"Gradually, step by step, with full conviction, one should become situated in trance by means of intelligence, and thus the mind should be fixed on the Self alone and should think of nothing else.

From whatever and wherever the mind wanders due to its flickering and unsteady nature, one must certainly withdraw it and bring it back under the control of the Self.

The yogi whose mind is fixed on Me verily attains the highest happiness. By virtue of his identity with *Brahman*, he is liberated; his mind is peaceful, his passions are quieted, and he is freed from sin."

New Testament Bible:

John 1:1

"In the beginning was the Word, and the Word was with God, and the Word was God."

Mathew 9: 35-37

"Jesus went through all the towns and villages, teaching in their synagogues, proclaiming the good news of the kingdom and healing every disease and sickness. When he saw the crowds, he had compassion on them, because they were harassed and helpless, like sheep without a shepherd. Then he said to his disciples, "The harvest is plentiful but the workers are few. Ask the Lord of the harvest, therefore, to send out workers into his harvest field."

Timothy 1:7

"For God gave us a spirit not of fear but of power and love and self-control."

Corinthians 4:5

"Therefore judge nothing before the appointed time; wait until the Lord comes. He will bring to light what is hidden in darkness and will expose the motives of the heart. At that time each will receive their praise from God."

Romans 11:36

"For from him and through him and for him are all things. To him be the glory forever! Amen."

Buddha:

Verse 167

"Do not live thoughtlessly, in distraction and with deluded aims, outside the universal law."

Verse 168

"Rouse yourself and follow the enlightened way through the world with energy and joy."

Qur'an:

Surat Al-Baqarah [2:256]

"Let there be no compulsion in religion: Truth stands out clear from error: whoever rejects evil and believes in Allah hath grasped the most trustworthy hand-hold that never breaks. And Allah heareth and knoweth all things."

Guru Granth Sahib:

Page 11

"Those who meditate on You, Lord, those who meditate on You—those humble beings dwell in peace in this world."

.~.

After Every Dark Night, the Sun Brings Light.

The Old World had to end; it was already dwindling in its existence.

Over the centuries, humanity had regressed from purity, truth, peace, love, and joy to stress, distress, misery, depression, anxiety, and mistrust...

It is time to bring Paradise on Earth because there is No other choice...

...and as we all individually transform, the New World begins...

10

The New World

The world is begging for a new beginning. It has to break the chains of complex entanglement and the stifling mental knots it has woven around itself, because these knots are not letting us live in peace, joy, harmony... However, a simple realisation that "We are what we think" suddenly creates a compelling reason to harvest gaps in our thinking to seek a higher platform to exist. Therein starts our realisation of our true self. In that "thoughtfully thoughtless" state we awake, and find the peace and joy inherent and inbred in our true self. And we find within all that we have all been seeking.

As freedom and liberty of our true-self, our soul, ensues from a stifling egoistic mind, we discover a fresh consciousness. Innocent and pure like a baby, connected with our creator, we perceive an amazing feeling of *TGIF: Thank God for Its Forever!* We are forever! And we are everywhere, because we are embodiments of universally prevalent energy that gives life to all beings. Through that energy we have unlimited access and connections with and to the entire universe. *We all are but one*!

This realisation unifies us with the acceptance of the Supreme Power and leaves us with a peaceful understanding. This understanding is sealed with unconditional love and righteousness, so that this access may not be misused by destructive elements. And in that supremely powerful realisation we are led to yet another truth, that is the code of conduct to live by: *another TGIF*. This would then have to be the essence of every being's life in the world of Paradise:

T- Total Truthfulness,
G- Giving Godly Love,
I- Invincible Compassion,
F- Full Focus in Present with Complete Faith.

TRUTH: Live in the truth, which is the present moment and think only truthful thoughts of what is needed in the now (and you may not need any thoughts in the now). Know your truest truth which is your soul, and The Ultimate Truth which is the Powers of the Universe, of which you are a part. By being truthful you are recognised as an integral part of the universe and receive the blessings of the entire Universe. This is often referred to as Grace. Hence, live like a protected CD; 'Corruption Denied'! Promote this principle by keeping company of those who do the same and send wisdom to those who are on their path to such a realisation. It is just a matter of time that everyone will be living in truth. Because, the truth is in intent, thought, word and action.

LOVE: The *only emotion our soul desires* is to experience is *"Love"*. It is a feeling of "Joy" and "Acceptance" put together and blended into a wonderful experience of belonging and fulfillment. In its peaceful, undisturbed and true original self, the soul already has complete acceptance from the super soul, the powers of the universe. So, even when no human reciprocates that emotion, one can receive it from that Super Soul in complete silence of a totally quiet mind. The soul can bask and fill itself with that "Love" and feel peaceful and be fulfilled. When one feels immense love in life what overflows from our being is a feeling of gratitude. By bringing this love in their own hearts, they can now give to others who need it. If one cannot find loving humans, it is better to be surrounded by loving animals than hateful humans, because we can only give what we have. Send love and compassion from afar to such people who are not *"Soul conscious"* as yet, and as a result show clear signs of hateful behaviour towards you. A genuine smile that lights up the eyes is the universal language of showing love towards each other.

But above all protect your Soul from harsh minds, because you first have to "Be One" with yourself before you can become one with another.

Provide yourself with unconditional love from your own inner source of life force, and communications and connections with Universal Energy and Power.

Other sources of agape love include spiritually tempered people, or if needed, loving animals and wisdom of God through scriptures.

Eventually, you may become so strong within that nothing can shatter your peace and joy, but initially remember "you can become the company you keep".

COMPASSION

"Treat others as you want to be treated". This simple concept needs to be the *basis of life.* If we apply this simple fundamental approach to all that surrounds us, we will bring back Paradise on Earth. It is the law of nature that you shall get what you give. So, if we want the best for ourselves we have to give the same to others. This is the barest essential principle in life that can replace the distress in relationships today with harmony.

FOCUS

Know that we cannot be at two places at the same time, and that if we are, then it is the tricks of the mind. The mind will attempt to separate us from our true identity, which is our soul, and in that state, our mind will compel us to make mistakes and suffer. So to remain in a peaceful, joyful, and blissful state; stay aligned in your body, mind and soul. In that state you practise with wisdom that pours out of your soul, and is sharpened by your intelligence. By being focussed in the here and now, and blending in and being one with everything around us, we are able to synchronise with the Universe. And by understanding and respecting the laws of the universe, we are able to live the best life possible.

FAITH

Once we know that we *(soul)* are immortal, and thrive under the grace of our Super Soul, the only intelligent way of living is by following the fundamental commandments of love and compassion in our interactions, with complete faith. Thereafter, we have no reason to fear or worry. Faith in the powers of the universe becomes the most wonderful perception in the world. The peace, contentment, and patience that come with this realisation are some of the most priceless qualities to have.

With that one word, faith, we progress from fear to fortitude, from fuming mind to forgiveness, from a perceived failure to complete fulfillment.

Going back to the simple answer suggested on page-44 in chapter three of this book regarding the transformation predicted by many, it has to be: *We just have to stop thinking unnecessarily and start being our true higher selves, in synchrony with all that surrounds us*! In that ego-less state of blissful union with the universe we are able to create our destiny with the co-creative powers of the universe, also referred to as *"Brahma Bhavati Sarathi."* This power of the Universe does not differentiate a soul based on any man made denominations.

.~.

The tragedy surrounding man today is that the very institution of religion engineered towards spirituality has taken man away from it. How can man meet his creator when he has built walls around himself and his fellow humans in the name of religion?

The most important understanding of current times is that irrespective of how many religions there are to practise, the Creator and Sustainer of mankind is ONE.

That Creator and Sustainer is neither Christian, nor Hindu, neither Muslim, Jewish, nor Sikh.

God, Allah, Bhagwan, Maalik, Almighty, Father in Heaven, Supreme Power, Universal Power, Ik Onkaar...are all names of the same Super-soul, from which all our souls originate and return to.

What we call this power is a mere nomenclature assigned by the limited human mind. To truly know it is to feel it, perceive it, and attempt to fathom it.

There are many titles imposed by man on what he perceives as God, and this division can be crippling and limiting if used for egoistic pursuits of superiority, power, greed, or violence. On the other hand, if we become united with that Power, it is in our best interest to receive its grace, irrespective of which religion we prefer to practise. Because only by that acceptance do we uplift ourselves to a life of bliss and fulfillment with wisdom and courage to pursue our purpose. Whether by birth or choice, whichever religion(s) we choose to pursue to realise that Power and through it our own, we *cannot* belittle another religion.

The very hallmark that a person demonstrates on reaching Union with the Supreme Power is that one loves and respects the Supreme Power and the entire creation of that Supreme Power, including another person's spiritual practices and faiths.

And just as one feels like a part of the Supreme Power, so is the entire creation a part of it. And through that common connection we all are a part of one another. What is there to hate or dislike? We just need to live with love and respect as members of one family: our family of one universe.

For those who don't realise this truth, they are unfortunately trapped in their ego-driven minds, unaware of their true identities and missing the very purpose of life: to be with peace and joy at all times.

.~.

One can compare the spiritual quest of man to a journey searching for a city, say San Francisco. We can take different highways to get there: 270, 101, 85, etc., but the important aspect is to get to San Francisco. If we get caught up in the choice of highway or get lost on the road or stay stuck in traffic, we may never get to San Francisco. *And the greatest need for this quest is to know ourselves better. Knowing our true identity is our birthright and is the only way to live with happiness.* Without this understanding, our lives will be a failure. We will think, talk, and act in manners that will repeatedly hurt us and others, making the whole world full of distress and misery.

But such a world of misery cannot exist for long. From times immemorial this "End of the World" has been predicted. These predictions are a testimony to the possibility of lack of faith in the human minds! Our minds are just not capable of delivering us to our originator or fulfilling the plan of immense joy we are intended to experience. However, a simple switch from the mind to soul conscious living can bring us back to our true intended life. In so doing, we find enjoyment in the present moment and avoid all suffering.

For as long as life has existed on mother Earth, there is only one most important aspect of our lives, and that is the only true power within us, the life force. This life force is capable of knowing the best and most appropriate way to live: in peace and joy with ourselves and harmony with our surroundings. This energy can keep our bodies healthy and help us in succeeding to the fullest as an embodied soul. After death we continue to exist, merging with the life force of the universe and vibrating in another form. This life force seeks only one language, and that is the language of love. It seeks only one dimension and that is of truth. Through love it desires to be connected to all that surrounds us with compassion. However, our complex lives have created a dominant force within us, our ego-mind. This "I and me" mind is full of nonsense stories of things that are not even happening in the present. But since our ego feels threatened all the time that it fills us with its stories to an extent that it completely shrouds the soul.

Even when we are physically in the present, our ego-mind takes us mentally far away and completely overrides our true identity, our life force, our soul. As a result, we lose all connections with the universe and become blind and powerless. It is as if we have to undertake a far away journey and someone disables our GPS (navigation system in the car). We have no clue where we are going, and soon we get lost. In that state we exist today depleted, distressed, and frustrated. And the simple solution is to just shake off the ego-mind—you do not need it. You will be able to use your observational mind, your intelligence, and even your instincts so superbly in the state where you are no longer a slave to the ego.

A new blissful and confident you will emerge, forever victorious. renewed and smiling. Thoughtfully thoughtless. Mindfully empty in mind and awake in awareness. Breath-takingly, fresh with every breath in the core of our being. That is our true nature, our true identity.

This true identity has been overshadowed by the blasting of unnecessary disturbing thoughts, that have no relevance to our truth or our present moment in life. Just a simple realisation of perceiving our soul with a quiet mind transforms our lives in a fraction of a second!

This state of awareness of our true selves, where there is stillness of the mind and joyous perception in the depth of our heart, has two distinct qualities:

1. A feeling of complete peace and joy,
2. Deep experience of unconditional love.

Unconditional love is when you love them irrespective of what, who, where, or how they are. Their joy becomes your joy.

This is the only feeling that the soul seeks, and it feels fulfilled when it finds it.

Therein it feels the peace and joy it deserves.

In that state we receive the wisdom of the universe to understand our purpose, the righteous path and are filled with courage to do what is needed.

Our thoughts, words, and actions become one with the universe and its creator.

These qualities empower us to instantly feel completely accepted. There is a sense of joy in just being. That feeling of acceptance and joy helps us to connect us with everything around us. By so doing we have access to infinite energies of the entire universe and its manifestation, and we have a knowingness of how to live in complete unity and harmony with all that is. In that moment, we all become one soul, as someone has appropriately said, *"Time is the soul of the whole world"*.

.~.

There can be more than one path to get a person to that state of unity with our higher self and the Higher Power. Irrespective of the path, the final practice and experience is the responsibility of each one of us, since each path only gives us knowledge. The application of that knowledge into practice is the wisdom we need to seek. The path does not matter; the goal, the destination is what counts.

And as we sincerely seek that state of awareness, the powers and energies of the universe further guide and bring about a transformation that brings about the fruition of that glorious, blissful goal. In that peaceful and joyous state we exist in unity with all lives filled with love and compassion, and it is evident in our dealings with others and the environment.

One can live by what the confused world tells us or by what our never-ending desires of the body prompt us to do or what the ever fluctuating, turbulent, and distress-prone mind dictates. As a result, man can exist anywhere in the spectrum from a selfish, animalistic, barbaric state to a Godly person.

But the most successful, peaceful, and joyful path is the one guided by the higher self, the soul. It is the quiet knowing of the righteousness that guides us in the stillness of our being.

And through it we are connected to the omnipresent and infinite universal energy, which helps manifest the most amazing realisation of our own infinite powers.

In that realisation and state of existence we are provided with the three jewels for the best life we can live with assured success: love, wisdom, and courage. And it involves only three simple steps of understanding:

1. *Self,*
2. *Supreme, and*
3. *Synergy.*

The simplest way to perceive the true self or soul is to silence the internal dialogue of insanity in the ego-mind, keeping the consciousness alert in the present moment, freeing the consciousness of unnecessary thoughts, and realising awareness beyond the thinking mind.

When the trio of self, supreme, and synergy connect in our lives, we will know that the beauty of life lies in its

simplicity, sincerity, serenity,

satisfaction, strength, service

As we elevate further into that experience, we feel an overwhelming sense of transcendence. Continuing in that state, one will experience deep joy and abundance in love in the core of one's being.

This is perceived as a patient, quiet, and confident knowing in the heart, not in the head, because the brain should be on a standstill with no thoughts. *This is the connection with the Supreme Universal Power, and through it we connect with all that there is.*

Everything around us becomes crystal clear, and suddenly we are one with all that there is; seen or unseen, manifest or unmanifest, obvious or hidden.

To solidify this experience, it really helps to recognise the footprints left by great souls and understands their realisations. Whether these are holy scriptures or wisdom of spiritual masters or psychological insights into the realms beyond mind, the effect of their influence is life transforming, definitely for the better! With that insight one will automatically seek to *simplify* their lives by prioritising and shedding unnecessary mind imposed burdens and focussing on the true relationships. These would come in the form of spouse, children and genuinely helpful and well-meaning extended family and friends who promote the feeling of peace and joy. Once we have found steady balance within ourselves, we will be able to help those in close proximity to us achieve the same for a harmonious life.

Similarly, the tasks we compel ourselves to do will also be streamlined to allow adequate time for work and relaxation. But irrespective of what we are doing or where we are, we will be filled with tranquility as we focus on each moment to the fullest without living in the false world of thoughts dealing with the past or future. Knowing the higher self and connecting with the higher universal power we lose all concerns about our imperfections or life's future perceived by our mind, which are mere perceptions and thoughts anyway! Neither are we bothered with any regrets of the past. And as we see others in the same light, we feel unconditional love towards everything and everyone and an overwhelming gratitude towards our creator! In that state we bring healing to ourselves and all those we come in contact with, and the world as a whole collectively stops creating disturbed minds. This is so because a lot of insanity is essentially caused by a lack of love and acceptance in an individual's life. The vicious cycle of hate stops and the cycle of love starts, transforming and healing the world...ushering in *The New World........*

And in the end only one word can sum up this realisation. It is a simple word in Sanskrit, which is used for greeting that says volumes:

Namaste:

(My Soul and Your Soul are one and part of the Super Soul, to that I bow with respect and adoration).

And so are the many others wonderful proclaims;

Shalom!

(Peace to All).

Amin!

(We pray).

Satnaam!

(There is only One Supreme, and it is Truth).

Bodhisatva!

(Enlightened Existence).

Amen!

(So be it, truly).

.~.

One of the Mayan Calendars.

Every moment

offers us an opportunity

for a new beginning. It is time to claim our birth-right and begin to live in complete bliss.

It is through each person's own inner power that they connect with the energy that has created and sustained the universe and now will transform their existences to eternal lives of infinite bliss.

Bibliography

Psychology by Charles G. Morris and Albert A. Maisto, Publisher: Prentice Hall.

Review of Medical Physiology by William Ganong, Publisher: Appleton and Lange.

Glencoe World History by Jackson J Spielvogel, Dinah Zike, Publisher: National Geographic McGraw Hill, Glencoe.

The Art of Yoga by BKS Iyenger, Publisher: HarperCollins.

The Holy Bible: English Standard Version, Publisher: Crossway, Good News Publishers.

The Holy Bible: New International Version, Publisher: Zondervan Publishing House.

The Holy Vedas by Debroys, Publisher: B.R. Publishing, India.

Bhagavad Gita As It Is by A.C. Bhaktivedanta Swami Prabhupada, Publisher: McPherson's Printing Group.

The Holy Gita by Swami Chinmayananda, Publisher: Thomson Printing Group.

Shrimad-Bhagwatam by A.C. Bhaktivedanta Swami Prabhupada, Publisher: Bhaktivedanta Book Trust.

The Holy Gita by Prabha Duneja, Publisher: Govindram Hasanand.

Handbook for Mankind by Buddhadasa Bhikkhu, Publisher: Thammasapa, Bangkok.

The Heart of the Buddha's Teaching: Transforming Suffering into Peace, Joy, and Liberation by Thich Nhat Hanh, Publisher: Broadway Books.

Zen Mind; Beginner's Mind by Shunryu Suzuki, Publisher: Shambhala, Boston and London.

The Noble Qur'an by On line Quran Project, Publisher: http://quran.com

English Translation of the Message of the Qur'an, by Dr Syed Vickar Ahamed, Publisher: Book of Signs Foundation, IL, USA.

The Signs of Al-Qur'an: Through the Prism of the Heart, by Saeed Malik, Publisher: Booksurge.

Sri Granth by Dr Kulbani Thind, Dr Sant Singh Khalsa, Jasjeet Singh Thind, Publisher: srigranth.org.

Holy Sunder Gutka by Ajit Singh Aulakh, Publisher: B. Chattar Singh, India.

Sri Guru Granth Sahib by Sant Singh Khalsa MD, Publisher:www.sikhnet.com/oldsikhnet/sggs/translation/sggstran2.html.

2012 (Mayan) Phenomenon by Foundation of Advancement of Mesoamerican Studies Inc. Publisher: http://www.famsi.org/.

List of dates for apocalyptic events Publisher: Wikipedia http://en.wikipedia.org/wiki/List_of_dates_predicted_for_apocalyptic_events.

Maya Decipherment by Dr David Stuart, Publisher: http://decipherment.wordpress.com/.

The Mayan Prophecy by Alex Whitaker Publisher: http://www.ancient-wisdom.co.uk/2012maya.htm.

The Mayan Calendar by Time and Date AS by Steffen Thorsen http://www.timeanddate.com/calendar/mayan.html.

Further Suggested Reading

Mind

As a Man Thinketh by James Allen, Publisher: Grosset and Dunlap.

Abraham Lincoln by James M. McPherson, Publisher: Oxford University Press.

Autobiography of Martin Luther King Jr by Clayborne Carson, Publisher: Warner Books Inc.

Mahatma Gandhi; His Life and Times by Louis Fischer, Publisher: Bhavan Book University.

Love, Medicine and Miracles by Bernie S. Siegel, MD, Publisher: HarperCollins.

The Power of NOW by Eckhart Tolle, Publisher: New World Library.

Practising the Power of Now by Eckhart Tolle, Publisher: New World Library.

Ageless Body, Timeless Mind by Deepak Chopra, MD, Publishers: Three Rivers Press.

You Can Heal Your Life by Louise L. Hay, Publisher: Full Circle.

Don't Sweat the Small Stuff by Richard Carlson, Ph.D., Publisher: Hyperion.

Meditations for Women Who Do Too Much by Anne Wilson Schaef, Publisher: Harper San Francisco.

The Enlightened Gardner by Sydney Banks, Publisher: Lone Pine Publishing.

Overcoming Wrong Mindsets [Audio CDs] by Joyce Meyer.

Body

Review of Medical Physiology by William Ganong, Publisher: Appleton and Lange.

Bio-chemical and Physiological Aspects of Human Nutrition by Martha H. Stipaunak, Ph.D., Publisher: W.B. Saunders, Div. of Harcourt Brace and Company.

Current Medical Diagnosis and Treatment by Editors Lawrence M. Tierney Jr., Stephen J. McPhee and Maxine A. Papadakis, Publisher: Appleton and Lange.

The Art of Yoga by BKS Iyenger, Publisher: HarperCollins.

The Encyclopaedia of Healing Foods by Michael Murray, N.D., Publisher: Atria Books.

Walking: The Ultimate Exercise for Optimum Health [Audio book] by Andrew Weil, M.D. and Mark Fenton, Publisher: Sounds True.

Soul

Near Death Experience Research Foundation by Jody A. Long JD and Jeffrey P. Long, MD. http://www.nderf.org/site_index.htm.

Many Lives, Many Masters by Brian L Weiss, Publisher: Simon and Schuster.

One Soul, Many Bodies by Brian L Weiss, Publisher: Simon and Schuster.

Communion with God by Neale Donald Walsch, Publisher: Berkley Books.

Mother Teresa; Her Life, Her Work, Her Message by Jose Luis Gonzale-Balado, Publisher: Liguori Publicataions.

Autobiography of a Yogi by Paramahansa Yogananda, Publisher: Jaico Publishing House.

Peace in a Restless World by Swami Chinmayananda, Publisher: Chinmaya Publications.

Meditations for Women Who Do Too Much by Anne Wilson Schef, Publisher: Harper San Francisco.

Siddharta by Hermann Hesse, Publisher: Bantam Books, Life of Pi: By Yann Martel, Publisher: Random House.

The Dalai Lama His Essential Wisdom by Editor-Carol Kelly Gangi, Publisher: Fall River Press.

The Gateway Experience (CD box set) by Laurie Monroe, Publisher: Monroe Institute.

Come Walk with Me by Carol Mayhall, Publisher: Water Brook Press.

Far Journeys by Robert Monroe, Publisher: Bantam Doubleday Dell Publishing.

The Five People You Meet in Heaven by Mitch Albon, Publisher: Hyperion.

Bold Confident and Fearless [Audio CDs] by Joyce Meyer, A Promise Fulfilled in a Dark Moment: By Dorothy E Stewart, Publisher: Xlibris Corporation.

Author's Childhood Spiritual Guides

Their message:

Live Truthfully

Be Happy

Work Faithfully

Love All

Trust God

Important Disclaimer

If the reader has any insights and realisations from reading this book, which brings into their life happiness and success, it is the result of their own fate and wisdom.

Please do not seek the author, who is just a messenger. Hence, the author would like to humbly remain oblivious.

A Family is God-ordained Institution of Love.

Each second is a snap shot of infinity.

Every cell participates in the energy of the moment.

When our entire being synchronises with all there is,

We melt and become one with the Universe.

Therein the manifest harmonises with the un-manifest, and in that state, Man and his Creator unite.